Two Sticks and a String

Knitting Designs Inspired by Nature

KERRY FERGUSON

Martingale
& COMPANY

BOTHELL, WASHINGTON

ACKNOWLEDGMENTS

THANKS GO TO

Stuart Ferguson, my husband and teammate, who has always been that great and solid rock upon which I could lean in times of doubt and that fountain of encouragement everyone needs;

Nancy Francescutti, the wonderful friend and knitter who has knitted so many of my designs into reality over the last fourteen years;

Michele Wipplinger, one of the world's leading colorists and proponents of natural dyes, who continues to inspire and encourage my journey in the stream.

To obtain yarns used in this book, contact:

Retail: *Northwest Peddlers*—1-800-764-YARN

Wholesale to the trade: *Creative Yarns International*—541-343-1932

CREDITS

President . . . . Nancy J. Martin
CEO/Publisher . . . . Daniel J. Martin
Associate Publisher . . . . Jane Hamada
Editorial Director . . . . Mary V. Green
Technical Editor . . . . Ursula Reikes
Design and Production Manager . . . . Cheryl Stevenson
Cover and Text Designer . . . . Trina Stahl
Copy Editor . . . . Liz McGehee
Proofreader . . . . Leslie Phillips
Illustrator . . . . Robin Strobel
Photographer . . . . Brent Kane

Fiber Studio Press is an imprint of Martingale & Company.

Two Sticks and a String: Knitting Designs Inspired by Nature
© 1999 by Kerry Ferguson
Martingale & Company, PO Box 118, Bothell, WA 98041-0118
USA

Printed in Hong Kong
04 03 02 01 00 99   6 5 4 3 2

The information in this book is presented in good faith, but no warranty is given nor results guaranteed. Since Martingale & Company has no control over choice of materials or procedures, the company assumes no responsibility for the use of this information.

Library of Congress Cataloging-in-Publication Data
Ferguson, Kerry,
Two Sticks and a string : knitting designs inspired by nature / Kerry Ferguson.
p.   cm.
ISBN 1-56477-262-4
1. Knitting patterns. 2. Sweaters. I. Title. II. Title: 2 sticks and a string
TT825.F45   1999
746.43'20432—dc21   99-20145
                                                                CIP

MISSION STATEMENT

We are dedicated to providing quality products and service by working together to inspire creativity and to enrich the lives we touch.

DEDICATION

OFTEN, IT IS a family that develops a creative spirit and keeps it alive. Mine is no exception. My mother, Millie Carol Kistler, took time when I was very small to teach me how to make clothes for my paper dolls and later taught me to draw fashion sketches. She loved well-designed clothes and never ceased to marvel at the ingenuity behind them. She was also very conscious of how clothes fit, and of the shapes and proportions that were the most flattering. Her enthusiasm ignited in me a desire to create my own clothes, and that desire has continued to develop.

As I was growing up, my father, Bill Kistler, often took me with him to his workplace, Vogue Printing Company, and instilled in me an appreciation for running your own business. His example showed me how hard you have to work to maintain customer confidence. He always went the extra mile for his customers, and many of them stayed with him for more than fifty years. Moreover, he never ceased to show confidence in my ability to tackle difficult tasks. That confidence abides with me even now.

When we took on the task of growing our yarn businesses, it was my husband, Stuart Ferguson, with his unfailing support and encouragement, who made the job a joy. His attention to detail and genuine pleasure in knowing our customers has been of inestimable value.

Now, a new generation is making its contribution. Our daughter, Chelsea Anne Loomis, worked with us after school and on weekends in our first Bainbridge Island, Washington, stores, where her sense of style and color and her genuine desire to help our customers were always appreciated. Now she has made her state an excellent territory for us by presenting our products well and meeting the needs of our customers. Her husband, Rob, has supported her by helping with their two children, often combining customer meetings and family outings. It is to Chelsea, too, that I first present each new collection, because I know she'll give me an honest and fair opinion as to what will work and what won't. Since early childhood, she has shown a gift for creating trends and styles, becoming a fashion leader from her first years in school. Our dialogues, debating size, proportions, color, and all sorts of details, are essential for maintaining my creative spirit.

Our two wonderful grandchildren, Austin and Madeline, continue to inspire me. It is great fun designing for them. Starting as babies, they have become great models for us, and I look forward to keeping them in sweaters for years to come.

This is what I mean by family—it's ongoing, and it's this constant nurturing that keeps the creative spirit alive and growing. To all of them, with constant thanks, I dedicate this book. They are all a part of it.

CONTENTS

Knitting in the Stream

Knitting has always held a special fascination for me. Not only does its rhythmic flow have a special appeal, with its patterns like K-P-K-P and K-P-P-K-P-P, but it also attracts me for another reason. When I pick up my needles to knit, I feel as if I were stepping into a stream that spans time and cultures and places. In this stream are all the knitters present and past, who used the same sorts of implements and materials that we use today to both clothe their families and express their creativity. When I step into that stream I become a part of it, too, knitting in the same way that has been used for centuries. Feeling that connection makes it a special experience. It is so marvelous that with only two sticks and a string a knitter can create shaped garments with all sorts of textures and colors. The designs can appear painted like landscapes or exhibit intricate textured patterns—without having to sew the pieces together!

As I began to design sweaters, first for myself and later for a wider audience, I found great satisfaction in working with ancient and diverse forms from a variety of cultures. This allowed me to connect with those who devised them, but at the same time, I felt compelled to put my own creative twist on them. In some cases, it was a method of design that I tapped into, as with the Arans and Argyles. I marveled at the way these methods had been honed over time to work easily with a minimum of hassle, so you could remember the pattern without referring to it all the time. Each detail has been thought out and revised until it works smoothly.

At other times, it was a strong visual image that caught my attention, and it became an exciting challenge to include that image in an original way. Though my designs echo my favorite images in these cultural traditions, I always try to use them in a way that brings a fresh expression to them.

In the designs that follow, feel the connections yourself. Step into the stream and imagine yourself carrying on a dialogue with all those who have contributed to the design, some far away in time and space, as you work the stitches and re-create the designs. Feel free to add your own creative spirit. Change colors, lengthen the design, shorten it, or use just part of a design. Above all, enjoy your time in the stream!

About the Author

Born in los angeles, California, as a fourth-generation Californian, Kerry Ferguson has always had a unique appreciation for the city and its environs.

She spent many hours with her family at the Southwest Museum, where Iron Eyes Cody sometimes acted as their guide, telling wonderful stories about life on the plains—the teepees, the beadwork, the buffalo hunts, and the tribe's ideas about life.

From an early age, she learned to appreciate the Hispanic community and its part in the early history of the area. She loved its lively and romantic music; its artistry with pottery, embroidery, silverwork, lace, and basketry; and its influence on the architecture of the beautiful missions and churches built by the Franciscan Fathers.

Kerry's mother, Millie Carol Kistler, was a marvelous designer who stopped work to raise her family, but never stopped sharing her enthusiasm and skills with her daughter.

Growing up in Southern California, Kerry couldn't help being influenced by the proximity of the movie industry. Edith Head, longtime costume designer for many major films at that time, became her idol. Like Kerry's mother, Millie, Edith was a master at proportion and fit, always making Hollywood's greatest stars look taller and slimmer than they were.

When she met her husband, Stuart, who had recently emigrated from England, Kerry renewed a childhood interest in knitting and needlework, spurred on by Stuart's fond memory of his mother and sister's needlework in his own childhood. She made blankets and sweaters for their daughter, Chelsea, when she was born and did needlepoint she had designed herself.

After graduating from the University of Southern California, Kerry taught in Malibu, Santa Monica, and Bel Air for seventeen years. Some of her fondest memories were of the school where she taught sixth grade in Santa Monica. It was a community where many families new to this country seemed to settle. She had the pleasure of teaching and getting to know students from forty-two different countries around the world, giving her a deep appreciation of the ways in which we are all alike as well as the beauty of our varied cultures and value systems.

Seeking a quieter pace and a more tranquil environment for their daughter to grow up, Kerry and Stuart pulled up stakes in 1981 and headed for the great Pacific Northwest, finally settling on Bainbridge Island, seven miles due west of Seattle by ferryboat. Here they bought their first store, which quickly established itself as a leader in the region. Called M.L. Mallard Ltd., it included knitwear design as part of its unique character from the start. Kerry began by offering her designs in their popular newsletter, and her customers responded enthusiastically. Several of them still have notebooks they have kept over the years, and it is not uncommon for them to bring in a newsletter from fifteen years ago and purchase yarn to make the design again because they've enjoyed it so much.

As time went on, Kerry and Stuart had the opportunity to entertain the great knitwear designers working in Great Britain, such as Kaffe Fassett, Sasha Kagan, Annabel Fox, and Sue Black. Kerry learned more about the art of designing knitwear from each one. Eventually, she published books of her designs with prominent yarn companies, such as Cascade Yarns, the Stacy Charles Collection, and Skacel Yarns.

In 1992, Kerry and Stuart introduced their own line of yarns, which became Creative Yarns International.

Their yarns came from New Zealand and were either completely chemical-free, such as their naturally dyed Bio-Spun Merino Wool, or otherwise processed in the most advanced eco-conscious way, such as their fiber-reactive dyed yarns and their newer Superwash. Even the buttons they sold were aimed at helping the environment. Hand carved of tagua nut from the Ecuadorian rain forest, the buttons have helped to develop a sustainable resource that retains the trees and harvests only the nuts themselves. Dyed with natural dyes in Seattle, they have been a consistent favorite for sweaters because of their light weight and soft colors.

As Kerry began to create books of sweater designs using their yarns, she found more and more expression for her earlier experiences with a variety of cultures. Not only did she gain a reputation for designing sweaters that fit well, but there was great enthusiasm for her use of ancient forms and images. In 1996, she was included in *Knitting in America,* a large collection of stories and works by some of America's best knitwear designers.

Today, Stuart and Kerry live in Eugene, Oregon, in the beautiful rolling farm country of the Willamette Valley, so they can be closer to their children and grandchildren and enjoy the richness of family life.

Basic Knitting Techniques

ON THESE PAGES I've outlined special techniques that make my knitting a satisfying pleasure. Use them, and yours will be too!

Gauge Swatch: It is essential to knit a swatch before beginning your project to make sure your garment will be the correct size. Using the suggested needles, begin by casting on the number of stitches for 4" plus 4 stitches on each side (to be worked in garter stitch). Work 4 rows in garter stitch, then the number of rows in the pattern stitch to measure 4" of rows, plus the 4 stitches on each side in garter stitch; then work 4 more rows in garter stitch. Surrounding your pattern stitches with garter stitches will make it easy to lay your stitches and rows flat so you can measure the center portion. If your piece is too large, try smaller needles. If your piece is too small, try larger needles.

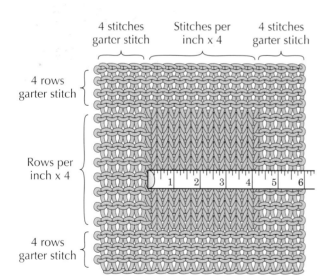

Gauge swatch

NOTE: Measure the full width of the garment piece after reaching 3" past any ribbing or edges to make sure your gauge is correct.

Fair Isle Technique: When two colors are worked repeatedly across a row, loosely strand (carry) the yarn not in use behind the stitches being worked. Always spread the stitches on your right needle as they are knitted to their correct width to keep them elastic. This will prevent the stitches from tightening up. Do not carry the stranded yarn over more than three stitches at a time; weave it under and over the color you are working. This will catch the stranded yarn in the back of the work.

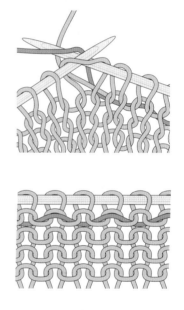

Full-Fashioned Decrease: Especially useful on V-necks and raglans. At the beginning of the row, knit 1 (K1), slip 2 stitches knitwise to the right needle one at a time; then with the left needle, knit both stitches together from the right needle (SSK). This may be done with purl stitches as well. At the end of the row, work to the last 3 stitches, knit 2 together (K2tog), knit 1.

Full-Fashioned Increase (M1): Particularly useful on sleeves. At the beginning of the row, knit 1 (K1); make a new stitch by lifting up the bar between stitches from front to back with the left needle and knitting into the back of the loop. At the end of the row, knit to the last stitch, M1, K1.

Knit Shoulders Together: Place both pieces on separate needles and hold them together with the right sides facing and the needle points at the same end. Then, with a third needle, the same size or larger, knit into the first stitch from each needle and knit them together. Knit the next stitch from each needle in the same way, then bind off (BO) the first stitch. Continue to knit one from each needle and BO until only one stitch remains. Break off the yarn, bring it through the last loop, then tighten.

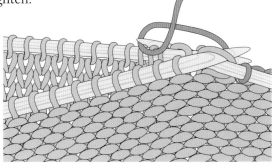

Picking Up Stitches: Pick up stitches from the right side of the work by inserting the right needle into the hole between the first and second stitch and drawing through a loop. Pick up the number of stitches per inch needed for the desired gauge, whether it is ribbing or another pattern stitch.

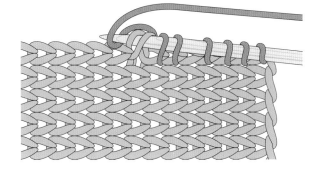

Intarsia: When changing from one large area of color to another, work to the end of the first color, bring the second color up from underneath so that it is twisted with the other strand, and no hole is left. Then, continue with the second color.

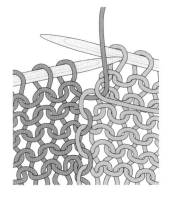

Kitchener Grafting Stitch: This is an invisible method of joining two pieces of knitting, either with the stitches on or off the needles, by exactly duplicating a row of knitted stitches.

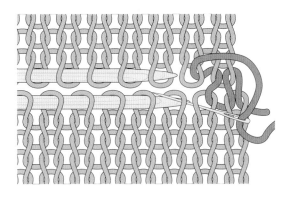

WEAVING SEAMS

Vertical Edge to Vertical Edge: Insert the needle under the horizontal bar between the first and second stitches. Insert the needle into the corresponding bar on the other piece. Continue alternating from side to side.

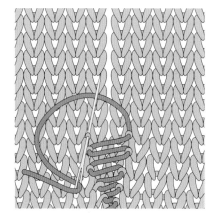

Horizontal Edge to Horizontal Edge: Lay out pieces, right side up, so that bound-off edges are facing each other. Insert the needle under a stitch inside the bound-off edge of the horizontal row. Then, insert the needle under a stitch on the opposite side and pull them together gently. Continue, working back and forth until all stitches are woven together.

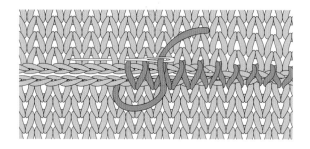

Vertical Edge to Horizontal Edge: Lay out pieces so the horizontal bound-off edge is facing the vertical side edge. Insert the needle under a stitch inside the bound-off edge of the horizontal row. Then, insert the needle under a bar between the first and second stitches of the vertical row. Continue in this manner, weaving as often per inch on the vertical edge as there are stitches per inch on the horizontal edge. This will sometimes mean skipping a bar at regular intervals or alternately, working under two bars instead of one.

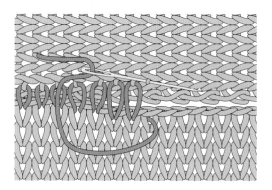

TERMS & ABBREVIATIONS

Garter Stitch: Knit every row.

Seed Stitch (odd number of stitches): *K1, P1; repeat from * across row.

Stockinette Stitch: Knit 1 row, purl 1 row; repeat. A reverse stockinette is purl 1 row, knit 1 row (the purl stitches face the right side of the piece).

BO	Bind off
CN	Cable needle (hook)
CO	Cast on
"e" wrap	Form yarn into a loop resembling the letter "e" and place it on left-hand needle.
K	Knit
K1B	Knit into back of 1 knit stitch.
K2tog	Insert needle into 2 stitches at once and knit them together.
M1	Full-fashioned increase (see page 7)
MC	Main color
P	Purl
P2tog	Insert needle into 2 stitches at once and purl them together.
RS	Right side
SL	Slip
SSK	Slip, slip, knit
St st	Stockinette stitch
st(s)	stitch(es)
TBL	Through back loop
WS	Wrong side
YO	Yarn over needle from front to back
YB	Yarn to back
YF	Yarn to front

NOTE: *Sometimes you will see these abbreviations in parentheses. Do everything inside the parentheses the number of times indicated outside the parentheses. For example, (K1, P1) 3 times means to knit 1, purl 1, then repeat 2 more times.*

Cheyenne
Saddle Blanket Jacket

ADVANCED

ONE SIZE

FINISHED CHEST: 68" · FINISHED LENGTH: 34"

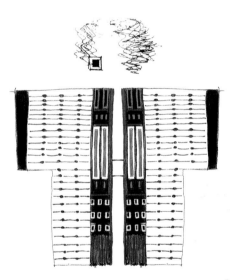

Inspired by a Cheyenne design for a beaded buckskin saddle blanket, this coat is an easy, oversized kimono style. The strong front panels are striking against the rhythmic bobbled stripes of the body. I knitted the color panels separately, which made the color work much easier.

MATERIALS

- 50-gram skeins (110 yards) of BioSpun Merino Wool by Creative Yarns International

Color		No. of Skeins
MC	Natural	15
A	Blueberry	5
B	Deep Red	2
C	Burnt Orange	1
D	Dawn Grey	1

- US 4 and US 6 needles or size to obtain correct gauge
- 5 large stitch holders

Gauge: 20 sts and 26 rows = 4" in St st on US 6 needles or size to obtain correct gauge

This pattern uses the following abbreviation to indicate a Make Bobble stitch:

Make Bobble (MB): K1, P1, K1, P1, K1 into same st, then pass 4th, 3rd, 2nd, and 1st st over 5th st.

BACK

WITH SMALLER needles and MC, CO 170 sts. Work in K1B, P1 ribbing for 7 rows, increasing 1 st on last row. Change to larger needles and work in St st for 8 rows.

Row 1: With Color A, K8, *MB, K13; repeat from *, ending MB, K8.
Rows 2–10: With MC, work even in St st, beginning with a purl row.
Repeat Rows 1–10 for pattern.
After 112 rows above ribbing, CO 40 sts at beginning of next 2 rows. Continue working in pattern until 198 rows are complete. Work Row 1 of pattern again. With MC, work 13 rows in K1B, P1 ribbing. Divide stitches onto 3 large stitch holders.

FRONTS

WITH SMALLER needles and MC, CO 44 sts; then change to Color B and CO 29 sts. Working in both colors, work in K1B, P1 ribbing, beginning with P1, and slip 1st st on each row that begins with B. Increase 1 st at beginning of 7th row. When 7 rows are complete, place 6 center edge sts on a holder. Change to larger needles and follow chart, increasing 1 st at center body edge as you begin, and working bobbles as on back. After 112 rows, CO 40 sts at sleeve edge. After 198 rows, on MC section, work Row 1 of pattern again as on back, then work 13 rows in MC in K1B, P1 ribbing. When all rows are complete, place all sts on a large holder. Work other front in same manner, but reverse shaping.

CUFFS

WITH SMALLER needles and Color A, CO 16 sts.

Row 1: Slip 1 st as if to purl, P1; *K1, P1; repeat from * across row.
Row 2: Work sts as they face you.
Repeat these 2 rows until piece is 26" long.
BO in ribbing. Make 2.

FINISHING

REFER TO Basic Knitting Techniques on pages 6–8.

Front Bands: With smaller needles, pick up front band sts from holder, increase 1 st at seam edge, and continue working in K1B, P1 ribbing, slipping edge st at beginning of every even-numbered row until band measures 32½". Weave band to front edge, easing as necessary so front band stretches to full length of body with just a slight bit of tension to keep it from drooping. Place sts on a holder with others. Work both fronts in same manner, but reverse shaping on second front.

Knit shoulders together. BO 20 sts across back of neck. Weave cuffs to sleeve edges so that slipped edge is away from seam. Weave underarm seams.

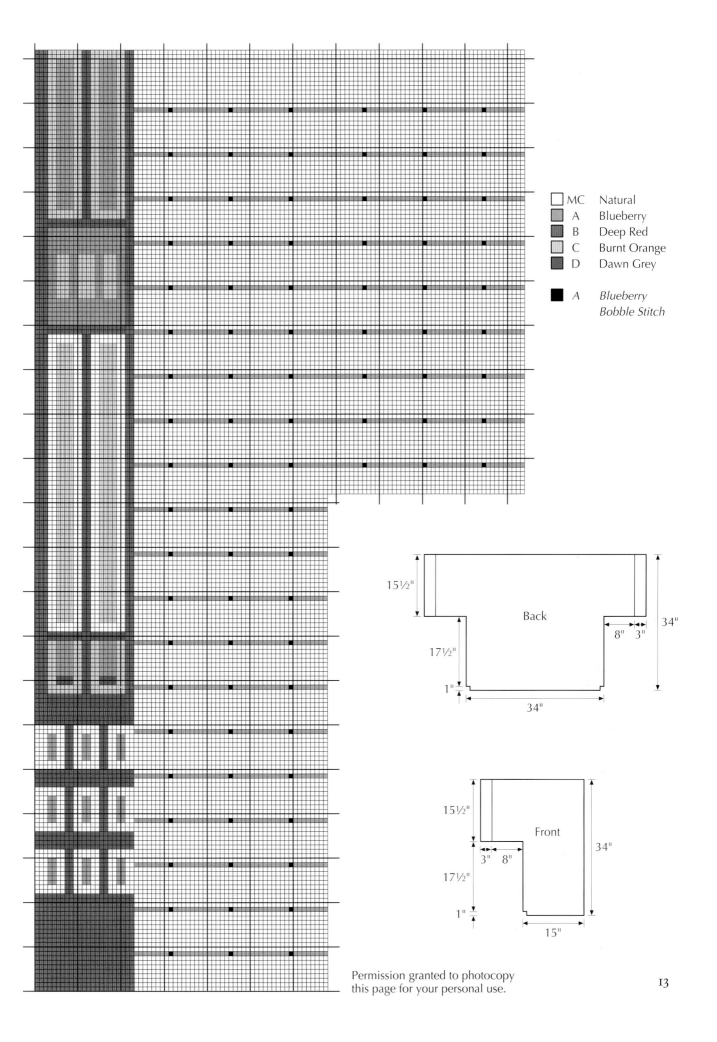

MC   Natural
A   Blueberry
B   Deep Red
C   Burnt Orange
D   Dawn Grey

A   *Blueberry
     Bobble Stitch*

Back

15½"

17½"

1"

34"

34"

8"   3"

Front

15½"

17½"

1"

3"   8"

34"

15"

Weather Dancer Cardigan

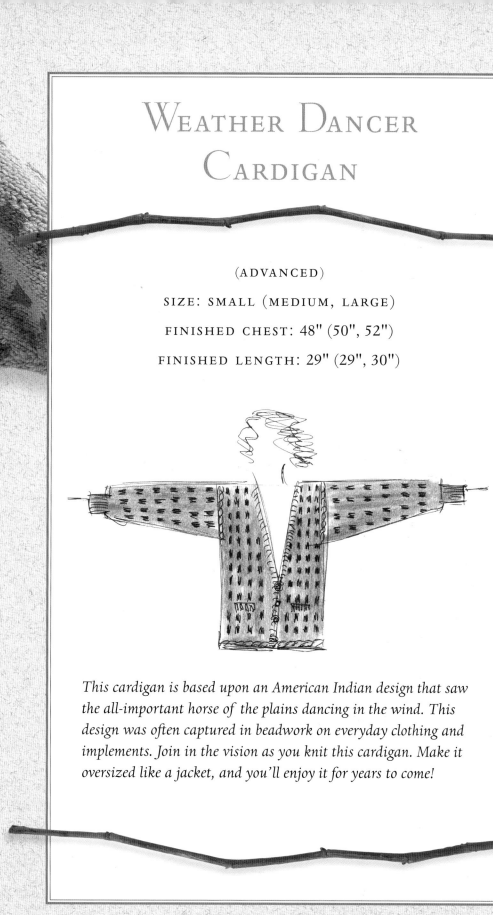

(ADVANCED)

SIZE: SMALL (MEDIUM, LARGE)

FINISHED CHEST: 48" (50", 52")

FINISHED LENGTH: 29" (29", 30")

This cardigan is based upon an American Indian design that saw the all-important horse of the plains dancing in the wind. This design was often captured in beadwork on everyday clothing and implements. Join in the vision as you knit this cardigan. Make it oversized like a jacket, and you'll enjoy it for years to come!

MATERIALS

- ✧ 100-gram skeins (160 yards) of Hearty Worsted 100% Perendale Wool by Creative Yarns International

Color		No. of Skeins
MC	Burnt Orange	8 (9, 9)
A	Grape	2
B	Wine	1
C	Plum	1

- ✧ US 7 and US 9 needles or size to obtain correct gauge
- ✧ Cable hook
- ✧ US G crochet hook
- ✧ 3 stitch holders
- ✧ Stitch markers
- ✧ 5 buttons, approximately 1" in diameter

Gauge: 16 sts and 20 rows = 4" in two-color St st on US 9 needles or size to obtain correct gauge (Using a larger needle will compensate for slight tension caused by stranding one color behind the other.)

NOTE: *For squares in main body of sweater and sleeves, use a strand of yarn approximately 20" long for each square, then weave MC behind it.*

The cable stitches in this pattern use the following abbreviations:

C6B: Slip 3 sts to CN and hold at back of work, K3, K3 from CN.

C6F: Slip 3 sts to CN and hold at front of work, K3, K3 from CN.

BACK

WITH LARGER needles and MC, CO 104 (108, 112) sts. Work in St st, following Weather Dancer Chart A. When vertical stripes are complete, work horse panel, except work first 9 and last 9 sts in MC as follows:

RIGHT SIDE CABLE
(Multiple of 6 sts + 3)

Row 1: K2, K6, P1.
Row 2 and all even-numbered rows: Work sts as they face you.
Row 3: Repeat Row 1.
Row 5: Repeat Row 1.
Row 7: K2, C6B, P1.
Row 8: Work sts as they face you.
Repeat these 8 rows for cable.

LEFT SIDE CABLE
(Multiple of 6 sts + 3)

Row 1: P1, K6, K2.
Row 2 and all even-numbered rows: Work sts as they face you.
Row 3: Repeat Row 1.
Row 5: Repeat Row 1.
Row 7: P1, C6F, K2.
Row 8: Work sts as they face you.
Repeat these 8 rows for cable.

When all rows have been completed, place sts on a large holder.

POCKET LININGS

WITH LARGER needles and MC, CO 22 sts. Work in St st for 4". Make 2.

FRONTS

WITH LARGER needles and MC, CO 49 (51, 53) sts. Work in St st, following Weather Dancer Chart B and working cable twists at shoulder edge as for back. Be sure to use full-fashioned decreases as explained on page 6. At Row 40, work 15 (17, 19) sts; work next 22 sts and place on a holder; then finish row. On next row, slip pocket-lining sts onto needle and continue. When all rows are complete, place remaining sts on a holder. Work both fronts in same manner, but reverse shaping on second front.

SLEEVES

WITH SMALLER needles and MC, CO 40 sts. Work in K1, P1 ribbing for 15 rows, increasing 10 sts evenly across last row. Change to larger needles, and work in St st, following Weather Dancer Chart C until all rows are complete. BO loosely with needles 2 sizes larger.

FINISHING

REFER TO Basic Knitting Techniques on pages 6–8.

CABLE STITCH
(11 stitches)

Row 1: Slip 1, P1, K6, P1, K2.
Row 2: P2, K1, P6, K1, P1.
Rows 3–6: Repeat Rows 1 and 2 twice.
Row 7: Slip 1, P1, C6B, P1, K2.
Row 8: Repeat Row 2.
Repeat these 8 rows for pattern.

Weave shoulders together. Weave sleeves to body. Weave underarm seams.

Bottom Cable: With larger needles and MC, CO 11 sts. Work in Cable stitch for 46" (48", 50"). BO in pattern. Weave edge that has 2 knit sts to bottom of sweater, easing it in so that it is under slight tension. Work 2 rows of single crochet along bottom edge.

Front Edge and Neckbands: With RS facing, smaller needles, and MC, pick up and knit sts along front edges and neck, skipping every 6th st and placing a marker at point of lowest neck decrease on buttonhole side. Work 2 rows in K1, P1 ribbing,

then on Row 3, work buttonholes as follows:

Work to marker; *BO 2 sts, work 18 sts, repeat from * twice; BO 2 sts, then finish row. On next row, make 2 "e" wraps over bound-off sts at each buttonhole. After 6 rows of ribbing are complete, BO firmly in ribbing, but not too tightly. Sew on buttons.

Pockets: With smaller needles and MC, pick up sts from pocket holder. Work in K1, P1 ribbing for 6 rows. BO firmly. Tack down. Stitch pocket lining down on inside. Work each pocket in same manner.

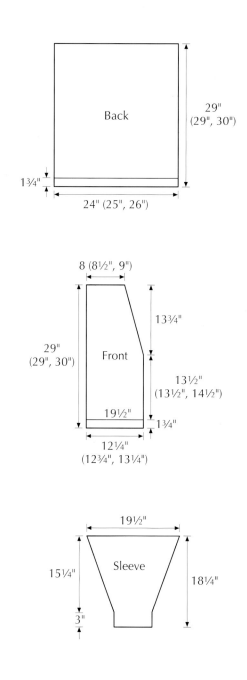

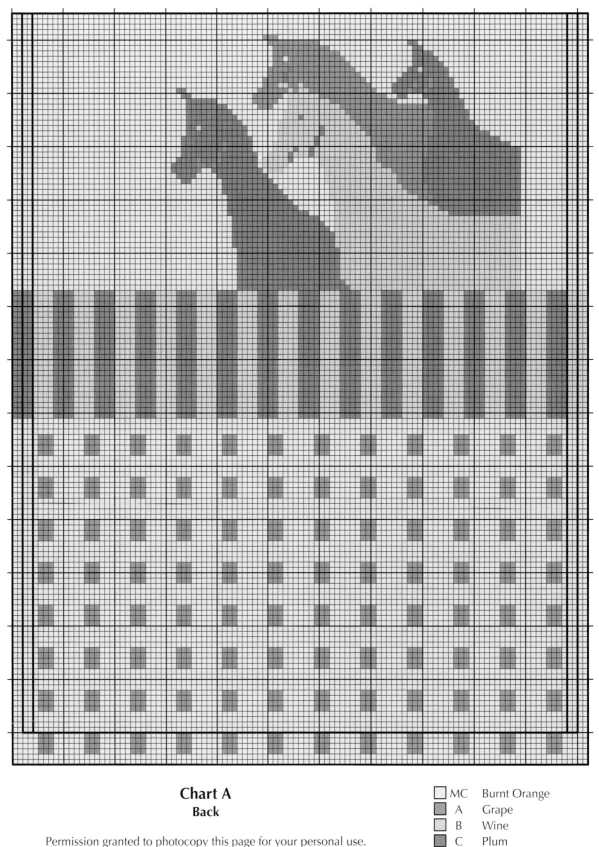

Chart A
Back

Permission granted to photocopy this page for your personal use.

☐	MC	Burnt Orange
▨	A	Grape
▨	B	Wine
▨	C	Plum

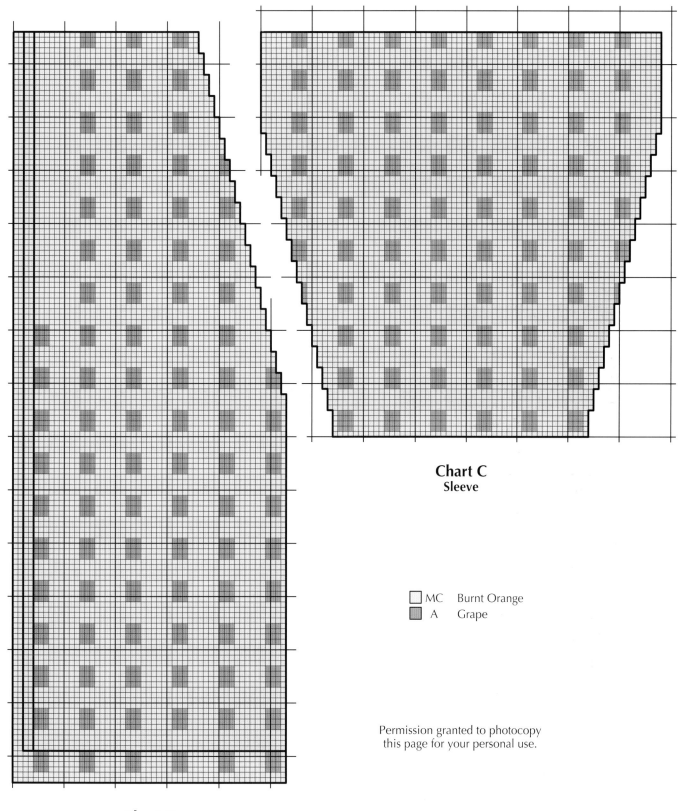

Chart C
Sleeve

□ MC   Burnt Orange
▨ A   Grape

Permission granted to photocopy
this page for your personal use.

Chart B
Front

Puzzlemaker Jacket

(ADVANCED)

ONE SIZE

FINISHED CHEST: 46"

FINISHED LENGTH

BACK: approximately 23" • FRONT: approximately 28"

Try this design if you dare to be different. It starts with one triangle and works its way around to the other side by a winding path that is full of little surprises, keeping this project fun from first stitch to last. And, it's all in one piece!

Based on the terra cotta and black glazed pottery of the New Mexico Pueblos, it utilizes a unifying stripe in garter stitch, with bouclé added for tactile interest.

MATERIALS

⚬ 50-gram skeins (110 yards) of Marina 100% Cotton

MC	Midnight Blue Grey	7 skeins

⚬ 50-gram skeins (125 yards) of 100% cotton bouclé

A	Terra Rosa	3 skeins

⚬ US 6 needles or size to obtain correct gauge
⚬ US F crochet hook

Gauge: 18 sts and 30 rows = 4" in garter st on US 6 needles or size to obtain correct gauge

TRIANGLES

WITH MC, CO 50 sts. Work from chart for Triangle A, slipping 1st st where indicated. When decreasing, work edge st at beginning or ending of row so that edge is straight. When all rows are completed, BO. Pick up and knit sts where shown for Triangle B. Work triangles in alphabetical order, picking up and knitting or casting on where indicated. Always count pick-up row as Row 1 of triangle. When all triangles are completed, BO.

FINISHING

REFER TO Basic Knitting Techniques on pages 6–8. Weave underarm seams. Work 1 row of single crochet rather tightly along back of neck.

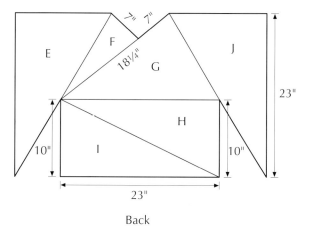

Back

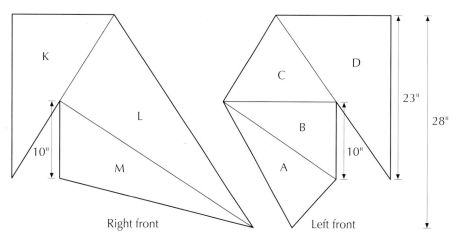

Right front   Left front

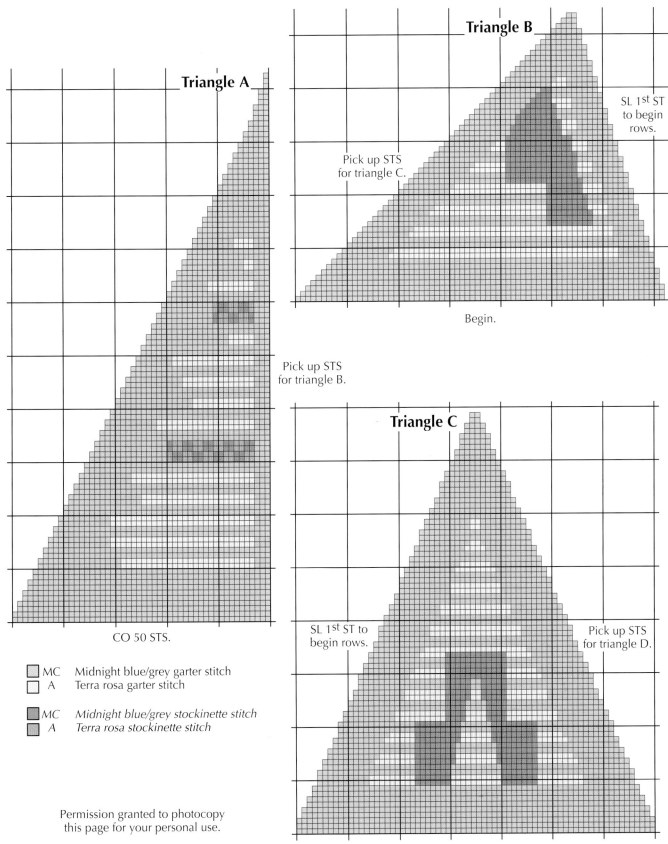

Triangle A

Triangle B

Triangle C

SL 1st ST to begin rows.

Pick up STS for triangle C.

Begin.

Pick up STS for triangle B.

SL 1st ST to begin rows.

Pick up STS for triangle D.

CO 50 STS.

Begin.

	MC	Midnight blue/grey garter stitch
	A	Terra rosa garter stitch
	MC	*Midnight blue/grey stockinette stitch*
	A	*Terra rosa stockinette stitch*

Permission granted to photocopy
this page for your personal use.

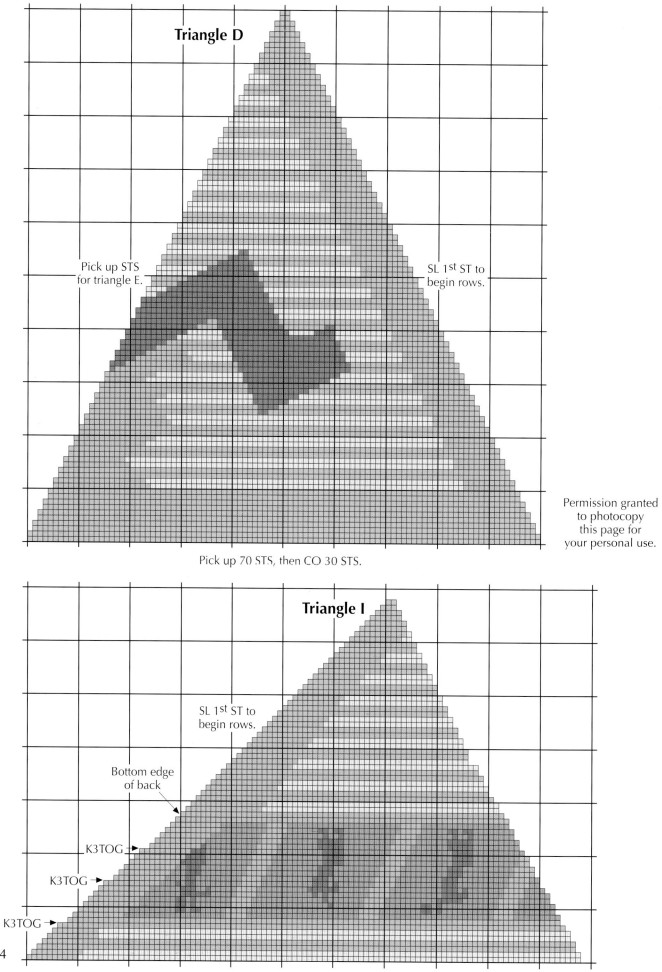

Triangle D

Pick up STS
for triangle E.

SL 1st ST to
begin rows.

Pick up 70 STS, then CO 30 STS.

Triangle I

SL 1st ST to
begin rows.

Bottom edge
of back

K3TOG →

K3TOG →

K3TOG →

24

Begin.

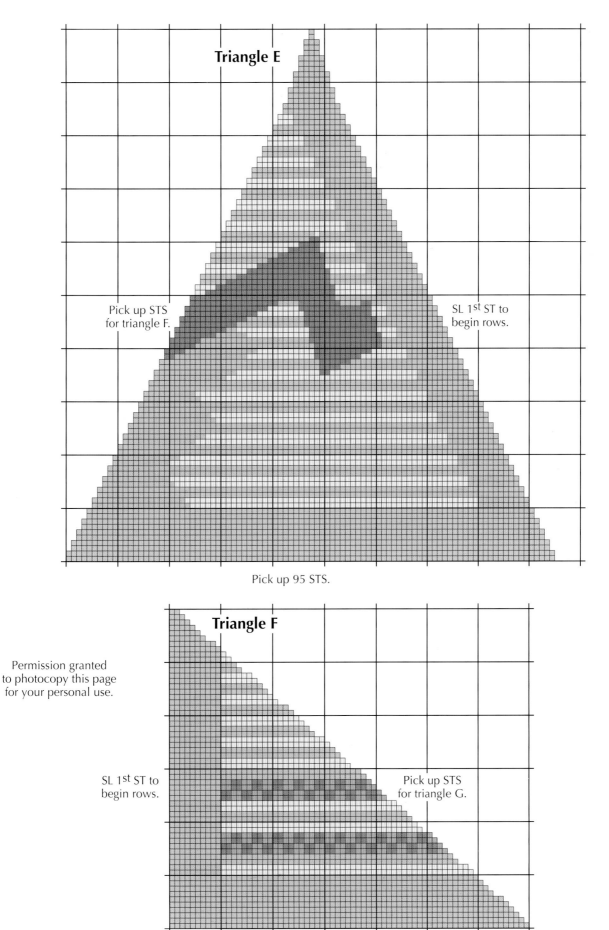

Triangle E

Pick up STS for triangle F.

SL 1st ST to begin rows.

Pick up 95 STS.

Triangle F

Permission granted to photocopy this page for your personal use.

SL 1st ST to begin rows.

Pick up STS for triangle G.

Begin.

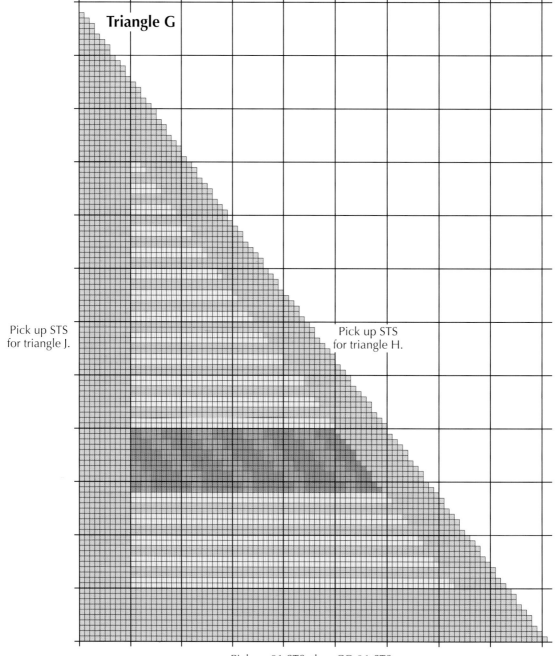

Triangle G

Pick up STS
for triangle J.

Pick up STS
for triangle H.

Pick up 91 STS, then CO 31 STS.

Permission granted to photocopy
this page for your personal use.

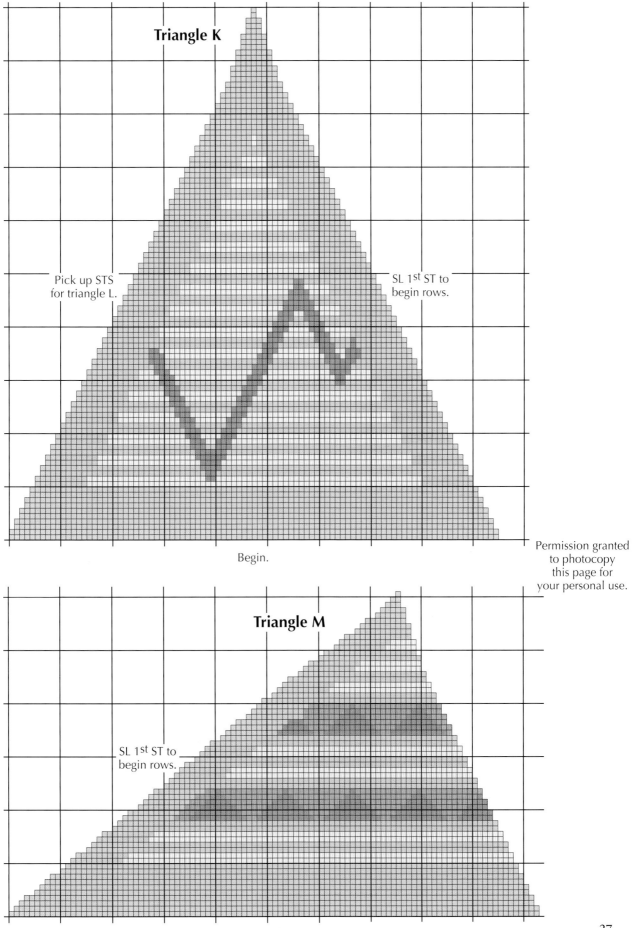

Triangle K

Pick up STS
for triangle L.

SL 1st ST to
begin rows.

Begin.

Triangle M

SL 1st ST to
begin rows.

Begin.

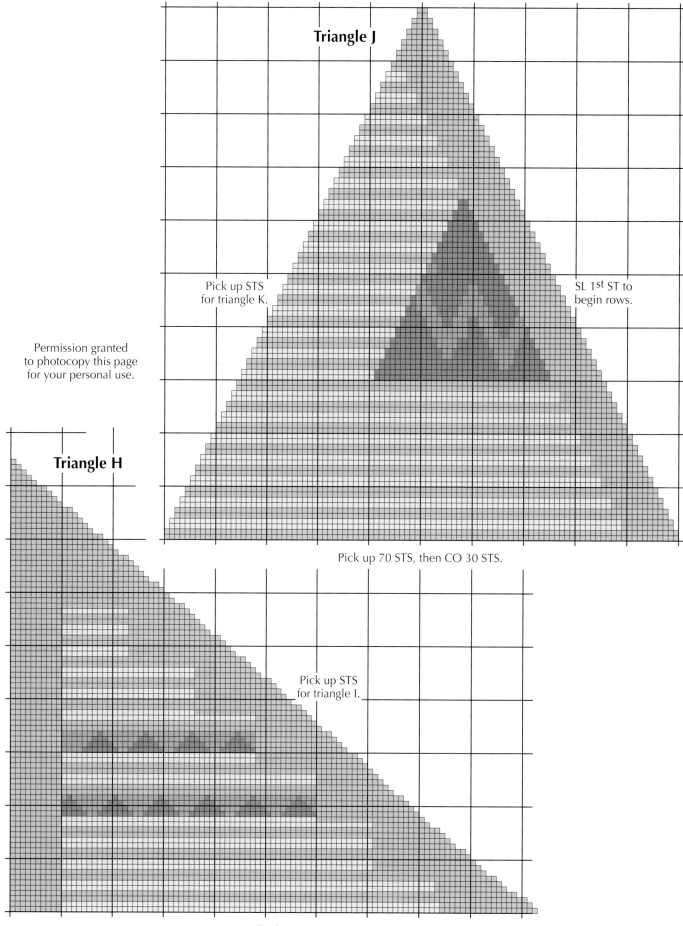

Triangle J

Pick up STS
for triangle K.

SL 1st ST to
begin rows.

Triangle H

Pick up 70 STS, then CO 30 STS.

Pick up STS
for triangle I.

Begin.

Triangle L

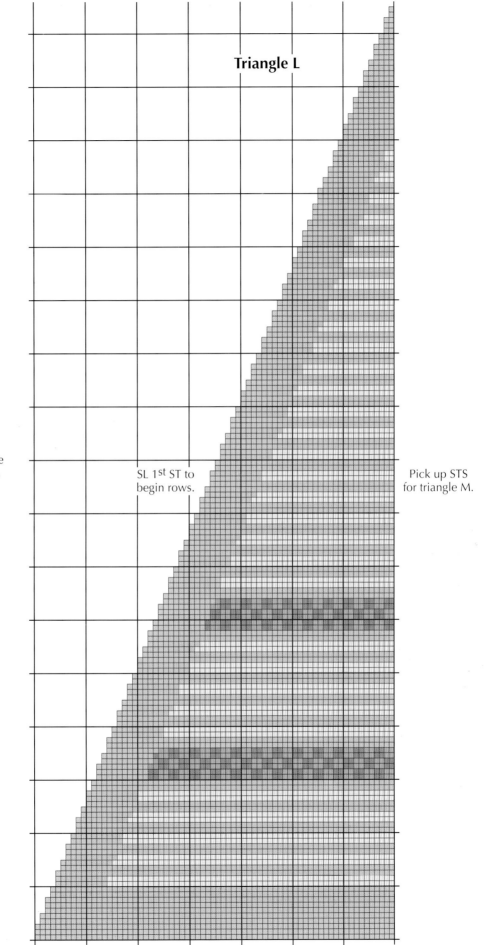

SL 1st ST to
begin rows.

Pick up STS
for triangle M.

Begin.

Aran Pullover

(INTERMEDIATE)

SIZE: SMALL (MEDIUM, LARGE)

FINISHED CHEST: 48" (50", 52")

FINISHED LENGTH

SHORT VERSION: 21" (22", 24")

LONG VERSION: 25" (26", 27")

This sweater is knitted in the tradition of the Aran Islanders: from the neck down in one piece. It's a very versatile design that can, with practice, be knitted in any size and with your own personal stitch arrangement. Knit one for every member of your family and they will wear them with pride.

MATERIALS

- 100-gram skeins (160 yards) of Hearty Worsted 100% Perendale Wool by Creative Yarns International

> 7 (8, 9) skeins for short version
> 8 (9, 10) skeins for long version

- US 5 circular needle (16" and 29") or size to obtain correct gauge
- US 8 circular needle (29") or size to obtain correct gauge
- US 5 and US 8 double-pointed needles or size to obtain correct gauge
- Large cable hook
- 4 stitch holders

Gauge: 18 sts and 24 rows = 4" in Double Moss stitch on US 8 needles or size to obtain correct gauge (Composite gauge of fancy stitches will be different, but if Double Moss is correct, garment size will be correct.)

FISHERMAN RIB
(Worked in round, multiple of 2 sts)

Round 1: *K1B, P1; repeat from * around.
Round 2: *K1, P1B; repeat from * around.
Repeat these 2 rows for pattern.

DOUBLE MOSS STITCH
(Multiple of 2 sts)

Row 1: *K1, P1; repeat from * across row.
Row 2: Work sts as they face you.
Row 3: *P1, K1; repeat from * across row.
Row 4: Work sts as they face you.
Repeat these 4 rows for pattern.

The Windblown Cable, Honeycomb Stitch, and Saxon Braid use the following abbreviations:

C2B: Slip 1 st to CN and hold at back of work, K1, K1 from CN.

C2F: Slip 1 st to CN and hold at front of work, K1, K1 from CN.

C4B: Slip 2 sts to CN and hold at back of work, K2, K2 from CN.

C4F: Slip 2 sts to CN and hold at front of work, K2, K2 from CN.

T3B: Slip 1 st to CN and hold at back of work, K2, P1 from CN.

T3F: Slip 2 sts to CN and hold at front of work, P1, K2 from CN.

T4B: Slip 2 sts to CN and hold at back of work, K2, P2 from CN.

T4F: Slip 2 sts to CN and hold at front of work, P2, K2 from CN.

WINDBLOWN CABLE
(Multiple of 14 sts)

Version One

Row 1: P2, C4B, P4, K2, P2.
Rows 2, 4, 6: Work sts as they face you.
Row 3: P2, K4, P2, T4B, P2.
Row 5: P2, T4B, C4B, P4.
Row 7: P2, K2, T4B, T4F, P2.
Row 8: Work sts as they face you.
Repeat these 8 rows for pattern.

Version Two

Row 1: P2, K2, P4, C4F, P2.
Rows 2, 4, 6: Work sts as they face you.
Row 3: P2, T4F, P2, K4, P2.
Row 5: P4, C4F, T4F, P2.
Row 7: P2, T4B, T4F, K2, P2.
Row 8: Work sts as they face you.
Repeat these 8 rows for pattern.

HONEYCOMB STITCH
(Multiple of 4 sts)

NOTE: *Be sure to use cable needle (CN) as directed on this stitch. It won't look right if it's worked like a twist.*

Row 1: *C2F, C2B; repeat from * to end.
Row 2: Work sts as they face you.
Row 3: *C2B, C2F; repeat from * to end.
Row 4: Work sts as they face you.
Repeat these 4 rows for pattern.

SAXON BRAID
(Multiple of 28 sts)

Row 1: P4; *C4B, P4; repeat from * 3 times.
Rows 2, 4, 6, 8, 10, 12, 14: Work sts as they face you.
Row 3: P3, T3B; *T4F, T4B; repeat from *; T3F, P3.
Row 5: P2, T3B, P3, C4F, P4, C4F, P3, T3F, P2.
Row 7: P2, K2, P2;*T4B, T4F; repeat from *; P2, K2, P2.
Row 9: P2, K2, P2, K2, P4, C4B, P4, K2, P2, K2, P2.
Row 11: P2, K2, P2; *T4F, T4B; repeat from *; P2, K2, P2.
Row 13: P2, T3F, P3, C4F, P4, C4F, P3, T3B, P2.
Row 15: P3, T3F; *T4B, T4F; repeat from *; T3B, P3.
Row 16: Work sts as they face you.
Repeat these 16 rows for pattern.

NECK AND SADDLE SHOULDERS

WITH SMALLER circular needle (16"), CO 112 sts. Work in Fisherman Rib in rounds for 2½". Place last 84 sts on a holder. Change to larger circular needle (29") and work first 28 sts as follows to set saddle shoulder pattern: K2, P1, K1, P2, K1; work 14 sts of Windblown Cable, Version One; K1, P2, K1, P1, K2. Continue in pattern, working cable as established and all other sts as they face you, until piece measures 10½" (11", 11½") in length. Place the 28 sts you just worked on a holder. Slip next 28 sts for the neck to a holder, then work following 28 sts for other saddle shoulder, using Version Two of Windblown Cable, leaving the final 28 sts for neck. When finished, place sts on a holder. Break yarn, leaving a 7" tail.

Aran Cardigan

(INTERMEDIATE)

SIZE: SMALL (MEDIUM, LARGE)

FINISHED CHEST: 48" (50", 52")

FINISHED LENGTH

SHORT VERSION: 21" (22", 23")

LONG VERSION: 28" (29", 31")

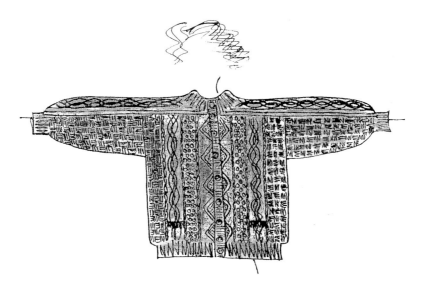

Step into the stream of history as you create your Aran Cardigan. You will be knitting it in the same way the Aran islanders have done it for centuries, from the top down. Don't be afraid to try a favorite stitch that will make it your very own.

MATERIALS

- 100-gram skeins (160 yards) of Hearty Worsted 100% Perendale Wool by Creative Yarns International

> 8 (9, 10) skeins for short version
> 10 (11, 13) skeins for long version

- US 6 and US 8 needles or size to obtain correct gauge
- Cable hook
- 4 stitch holders
- 7 (10 for long version) Natural Tagua Nut buttons by Creative Yarns International, 1" diameter

Gauge: 18 sts and 22 rows = 4" in Double Moss stitch on US 8 needles or size to obtain correct gauge (Composite gauge of varied stitches will be different, but if Double Moss is correct, the garment size will be correct.)

DOUBLE MOSS STITCH
(Multiple of 2 sts)

Row 1: *K1, P1; repeat from * across row.
Row 2: Work sts as they face you.
Row 3: *P1, K1; repeat from * across row.
Row 4: Work sts as they face you.
Repeat these 4 rows for pattern.

TRIPLE CROSS
(Multiple of 3 sts)

Row 1: K3.
Row 2: Work sts as they face you.
Row 3: Skip 1st st, K2, then knit first st.
Row 4: Work sts as they face you.
Repeat these 4 rows for pattern.

The Double Wave Cable, Trinity Stitch, and Aran Half-Diamonds use the following abbreviations:
C4B: Slip 2 sts to CN and hold at back of work, K2, K2 from CN.
C4F: Slip 2 sts to CN and hold at front of work, K2, K2 from CN.
M3: K1, P1, K1 into next st.
T3B: Slip 1 st to CN and hold at back of work, K2, P1 from CN.
T3F: Slip 2 sts to CN and hold at front of work, P1, K2 from CN.

DOUBLE WAVE CABLE
(Multiple of 16 sts)

Row 1: K2, P3, K2, P2, K2, P3, K2.
Row 2 and all even-numbered rows: Work sts as they face you.
Row 3: T3F, P2, T3F; T3B, P2, T3B.
Row 5: P1, T3F; P2; C4F, P2, T3B, P1.
Row 7: P2, (T3F, T3B) twice, P2.
Row 9: P3, C4F, P2, C4F, P3.
Row 11: P2, (T3B, T3F) twice, P2.
Row 13: P1, T3B, P2, C4F, P2, T3F, P1.
Row 15: T3B, P2, T3B, T3F, P2, T3F.
Row 16: Repeat Row 2.
Rows 17–32: Repeat Rows 1–16, but work C4B instead of C4F in 5th, 9th, and 13th rows.
Repeat these 32 rows for pattern.

TRINITY STITCH
(Multiple of 4 sts + 2)

Row 1: Purl.
Row 2: K1; *M3, P3tog; repeat from * to last st; K1.
Row 3: Purl.
Row 4: K1; *P3tog, M3; repeat from * to last st; K1.
Repeat these 4 rows for pattern.

RIGHT ARAN HALF-DIAMOND
(Multiple of 7 sts)

Row A (worked only once): P5, K2
Row 1: P2, K5.
Row 2: P4, T3B.
Row 3 and all other odd-numbered rows: Work
   sts as they face you.
Row 4: P3, T3B, K1.
Row 6: P2, T3B, K1, P1.
Row 8: P1, T3B, K1, P1, K1.
Row 10: T3B, (K1, P1) twice.
Row 12: T3F, (P1, K1) twice.
Row 14: P1, T3F, P1, K1, P1.
Row 16: P2, T3F, P1, K1.
Row 18: P3, T3F, P1.
Row 20: P4, T3F.
Repeat Rows 1–20 for pattern.

LEFT ARAN HALF-DIAMOND
(Multiple of 7 sts)

Row A (worked only once): K2, P5.
Row 1: K5, P2.
Row 2: T3F, P4.
Row 3 and all other odd-numbered rows: Work
   sts as they face you.
Row 4: K1, T3F, P3.
Row 6: P1, K1, T3F, P2.
Row 8: K1, P1, K1, T3F, P1.
Row 10: (P1, K1) twice, T3F.
Row 12: (K1, P1) twice, T3B.
Row 14: P1, K1, P1, T3B, P1.
Row 16: K1, P1, T3B, P2.
Row 18: P1, T3B, P3.
Row 20: T3B, P4.
Repeat Rows 1–20 for pattern.

ARAN DIAMONDS WITH MOSS STITCH
(Multiple of 13 sts)

*BC (Back Cross): Slip 1 st to CN and hold in back, K1B,
   P1 from CN.*
*FC (Front Cross): Slip 1 st to CN and hold in front, P1,
   K1B from CN.*

Row 1: P5; slip next 2 sts to CN and hold in front,
   K1B, then slip 1 purl st from CN to left-hand
   needle and purl it, K1B from CN; P5.
Row 2: K5, P1, K1, P1, K5.
Row 3: P4, BC, K1, FC, P4.
Row 4 and all other even-numbered rows: Work
   sts as they face you.
Row 5: P3, BC, K1, P1, K1, FC, P3.
Row 7: P2, BC, (K1, P1) twice, K1, FC, P2.
Row 9: P1, BC, (K1, P1) 3 times, K1, FC, P1.
Row 11: BC, (K1, P1) 4 times, K1, FC.
Row 13: FC, (P1, K1) 4 times, P1, BC.
Row 15: P1, FC, (P1, K1) 3 times, P1, BC, P1.
Row 17: P2, FC, (P1, K1) twice, P1, BC, P2.
Row 19: P3, FC, P1, K1, P1, BC, P3.
Row 21: P4, FC, P1, BC, P4.
Row 22: Repeat Row 2.
Repeat these 22 rows for pattern.

NECK AND SADDLE SHOULDERS

WITH SMALLER needles, CO 99 sts. Work in K1B, P1 ribbing for 6". Place 10 sts on a holder; leave next 30 sts on needle; place remaining 59 sts on a holder. Change to larger needles and work 30 sts on needle as follows: K2, P2, K1B, P2; work 16 sts in Double Wave Cable; P2, K1B, P2, K2. Continue, working sts on either side of cable as they face you. Work until piece measures 10" (10½", 11") long from ribbing. Place sts on a holder. Return to stitch holder with 59 sts. Place 19 sts for back on a holder, 30 sts on needles, and 10 sts on a holder. Work 30 sts on needles in same manner as other shoulder. Break yarn.

LEFT FRONT

WITH RS facing, pick up and knit 10 neck sts from holder. Working along the saddle shoulder edge, pick up and knit 51 (53, 55) sts between the 1st row of edge sts and the next row. Break yarn so 1st row can be a right-side row. Set up pattern as follows: K2, work 7 sts in Left Aran Half-Diamond; work 3 sts in Triple Cross; work 14 sts in Trinity stitch; work 3 sts in Triple Cross; P2, work 16 sts in Double Wave Cable; P2, work 3 sts in Triple Cross; work 7 (9, 11) sts in Double Moss stitch, K2. Continue, working established patterns and all non-pattern sts as they face you. Continue until piece measures 8½" long from pick-up row. Place sts on a holder.

RIGHT FRONT

WORK RIGHT front in same manner as left front, reversing sequence and using Right Aran Half-Diamond.

BACK

WITH RS facing, pick up and knit 117 (121, 125) sts, including 19 sts from holder. Once again, break yarn and work 1st row of pattern (right-side row) as follows: K2, work 7 (9, 11) sts in Double Moss; work 3 sts in Triple Cross; P2, work 16 sts in Double Wave Cable; work 3 sts in Triple Cross; work 14 sts in Trinity stitch; work 3 sts in Triple Cross; work 15 sts in Aran Diamonds with Moss stitch; work 3 sts in Triple Cross; work 14 sts in Trinity stitch; work 3 sts in Triple Cross; P2, work 16 sts in Double Wave Cable; P2, work 3 sts in Triple Cross; work 7 (9, 11) sts in Double Moss stitch, K2. Continue, working established patterns and non-pattern sts as they face you. Continue until back measures same length as fronts.

SLEEVES

BEGINNING AT underarm with RS facing and larger needles, pick up and knit 38 sts along armhole edge, working between 1st and 2nd st and skipping approximately every 5th st. Work across sts on holder in pattern. Pick up 38 sts on back armhole edge, again skipping approximately every 5th st. Work in rounds or flat. Working sts on either side of shoulder cable in Double Moss stitch and continuing established saddle shoulder pattern, work even for 3". Continue in pattern, decreasing on either side of an imaginary underarm seam every 4th row until sleeve measures 14" in total length. When decreasing, be sure to use full-fashioned decreases (see page 6). Decrease to 46 sts across next row; then change to smaller needles. Work in K1B, P1 ribbing, alternating with rounds of K1, P1B if working in the round, for 3". BO in ribbing.

COMPLETING FRONTS AND BACK

PLACE FRONTS and back together on one needle. Continue working all established patterns, but knit the 2 edge sts together at each armhole to make a panel of Triple Cross, increasing between the 2 sts to make 3 for pattern. Continue until length for pocket is reached, 16" from center of saddle shoulder for short version, 18" for long version. End ready for a right-side row. Work 29 (31, 33) sts; work 20 sts and place on a holder; work to last 49 (51, 53) sts; work 20 sts and place on a holder; work 29 (31, 33) sts. On next row, CO 20 sts across each holder and continue in pattern until piece measures 19" (20", 21") from center of saddle shoulder for short version, 25" (26", 28") for long version. Change to smaller needles and work in K1B, P1 ribbing for 2" (short version) or 3" (long version). BO in ribbing.

FINISHING

REFER TO Basic Knitting Techniques on pages 6–8. Tack down collar on inside.

Front Bands: With RS facing and smaller needles, pick up and knit sts along left front edge, skipping approximately every 5th st. Work in K1B, P1 ribbing for 2 rows. In next row, work 7 buttonholes for short version, or 10 buttonholes for long version, placing one 1" from bottom, then approximately 3" apart, ending with one 1" from top. Make buttonholes as follows: Work to buttonhole; *BO 2 sts, CO 2 sts over them with a simple "e" loop cast-on, continue to next buttonhole; repeat from * until all buttonholes are made. Work 2 more rows, then BO firmly. Work other band in same manner, but without buttonholes. Sew on buttons.

Pockets: Pick up pocket sts from holders and work 3½" of pocket lining in pattern. BO in pattern. Tack down. Pick up cast-on sts and work 5 rows of K1B, P1 ribbing. BO in ribbing. Tack down.

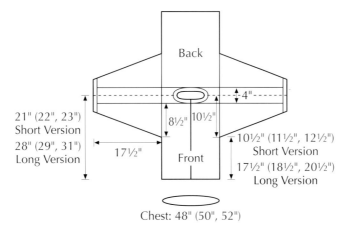

21" (22", 23")
Short Version
28" (29", 31")
Long Version

Back

4"

8½" 10½"

17½"

Front

10½" (11½", 12½")
Short Version
17½" (18½", 20½")
Long Version

Chest: 48" (50", 52")

HANDS-ACROSS-THE-WORLD JACKET

ADVANCED

SIZE: SMALL (MEDIUM, LARGE)

FINISHED CHEST: 40" (43", 46")

FINISHED LENGTH: 20" (21½", 23")

In honor of greater peace in the world and the 1992 summer Olympics in Barcelona, Spain, this great-fitting jacket features the flags of thirty-two countries. Pick your favorites for your own version.

MATERIALS

⚭ 50-gram skeins (109 yards) of 100% cotton

Color		No. of Skeins
MC	Red	10 (11, 12)
A	Green	2
B	Yellow	2
C	Sky Blue	2
D	Pink	2
E	Navy	1
F	Natural	1
G	Brown	1
H	Goldenrod	1
I	Peach	1
J	Persimmon	1
K	Ebony	1

⚭ US 3 and US 4, 5, or 6 needles (depending on size of garment) or size to obtain correct gauge

⚭ 8 stitch holders

⚭ 1 ball of gold metallic yarn in double-knitting (DK) weight

⚭ 6 buttons, ½" diameter

Gauge

For Small (23 sts, 28 rows) = 4" in St st on US 4 needle or size to obtain correct gauge

For Medium (22 sts, 26 rows) = 4" in St st on US 5 needle or size to obtain correct gauge

For Large (20 sts, 24 rows) = 4" in St st on US 6 needle or size to obtain correct gauge

RIDGE PATTERN

Rows 1, 3, 5: Knit.
Rows 2, 4: Purl.
Row 6: Knit.
Repeat these 6 rows for pattern.

DOUBLE MOSS STITCH

(Multiple of 2 sts)

Row 1: *K1, P1; repeat from * across row.
Row 2: Work sts as they face you.
Row 3: *P1, K1; repeat from * across row.
Row 4: Work sts as they face you.
Repeat these 4 rows for pattern.

BACK

WITH SMALLER needles and MC, CO 116 sts. Working in garter st, work 4 rows in MC, 4 rows in B, and 4 rows in C. Change to larger needles and follow Chart A for back. See Basic Knitting Techniques on pages 6–8 for working multicolor sections. Work all stripe rows (Color D) in garter st. When all rows are completed, place all sts on a large holder.

RIGHT FRONT

WITH SMALLER needles and MC, CO 63 sts. Work first 12 rows as for back, slipping 1st st knitwise on all odd-numbered rows and working a buttonhole on Rows 6 and 7 as follows:

Row 6: Work to last 4 sts, YO, K2tog, finish row.
Row 7: Slip 1, K1, knit the YO, finish row.

After bottom band is complete, change to larger needles. Place first 7 sts on a holder and work remaining sts, following Chart B for right front. Stop 6 rows from top and shape neck. Place first 5 sts on holder and continue in pattern, decreasing at neck edge every other row 3 times. Place remaining sts on a holder.

LEFT FRONT

WORK AS for right front but reverse shaping and omit buttonhole. Follow Chart C for left front.

SLEEVES

WITH SMALLER needles and MC, CO 64 sts. Work 4 rows of garter st in MC, 4 rows in B, and 4 rows in C. Change to larger needles and MC. Set up pattern as follows:

*K1, P1; repeat from * 4 times; K44; **P1, K1, repeat from ** 4 times.

Continue in pattern, working side sections in Double Moss stitch and center section in Ridge pattern.

Increase 1 st each side every 5th row 20 times (104 sts), working new sts into Double Moss stitch. Beginning with next row, work all sts in Ridge pattern, increasing 1 st each side every 5th row 2 times. When sleeve measures 16" in length, place Double Moss side panel sts on holders and work center 44 sts for 6½" more. End ready for a right-side row. Divide for neck.

Work 22 sts. BO 5 sts. Start a new ball of yarn. Finish row. Work 1 row. On next row, BO 6 sts; finish row. Work 1 row. On next row, BO 5 sts; finish row. Work 1 row. On next row, BO remaining 6 sts. Return to remaining sts. Work 3½" more. Place sts on holders. Work second sleeve in same manner as first, but reverse shaping.

FINISHING

REFER TO Basic Knitting Techniques on pages 6–8.
Using kitchener grafting stitch, attach sleeves to back and fronts. Weave underarm seams, matching all stripes.

Front Bands: On right front, pick up band sts from holder with smaller needles. Increase 1 st on edge closest to body. Work in garter st, slipping outside edge st when beginning a row, working stripes as established and working buttonholes as before where desired. (One will be placed in neckband.) Continue until front band is approximately 1" shorter than front body. End with MC or Color B. Work left front band in same manner, but without buttonholes. Weave bands to front edge, easing as necessary so front band stretches to full length of body with just a slight bit of tension. Sew on buttons.

Neckband: With RS facing, smaller needles, and Color C, pick up and knit sts from right front band, sts from holder, sts from side neck, sts from back of neck, sts from other side neck, sts from other holder, then sts from other front band. Knitting back and forth in garter st, work 3 more rows of Color C, 4 rows of Color B, and 4 rows of MC, placing a buttonhole in middle 2 rows of B. When all rows are completed, BO.

Weave all ends in carefully, knotting ends to discourage them from working loose. With gold metallic yarn, work a row of stem stitch around edge of each flag. This gives polish to your masterpiece!

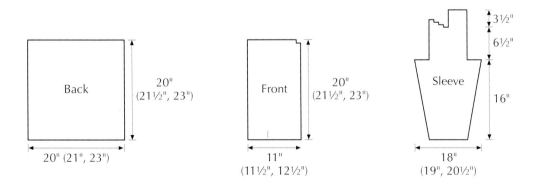

Stem Stitch

Back
20" (21½", 23")
20" (21", 23")

Front
20" (21½", 23")
11" (11½", 12½")

Sleeve
3½"
6½"
16"
18" (19", 20½")

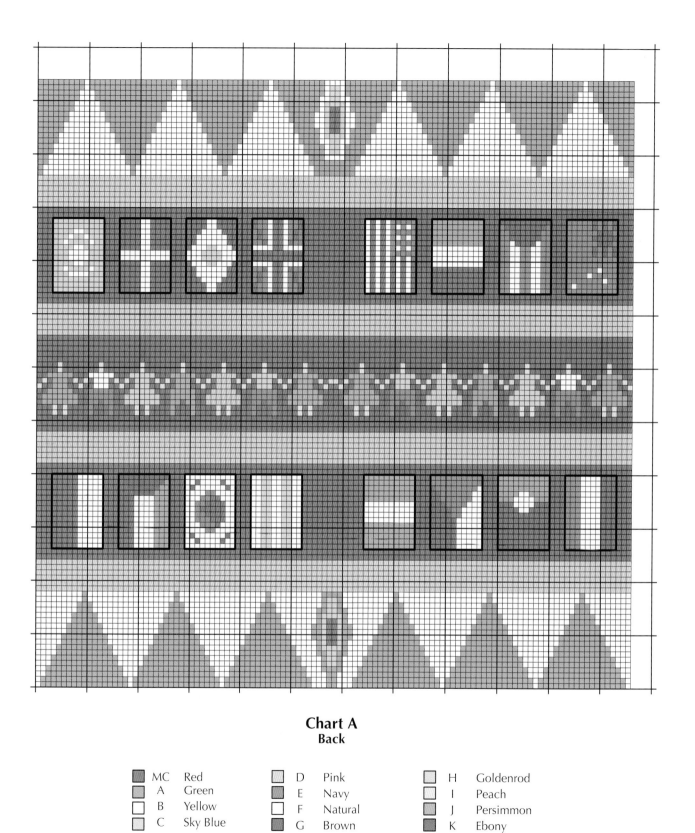

Chart A
Back

▨ MC	Red	▨ D	Pink	▨ H	Goldenrod
▨ A	Green	▨ E	Navy	▨ I	Peach
□ B	Yellow	□ F	Natural	▨ J	Persimmon
▨ C	Sky Blue	▨ G	Brown	▨ K	Ebony

Permission granted to photocopy this page for your personal use.

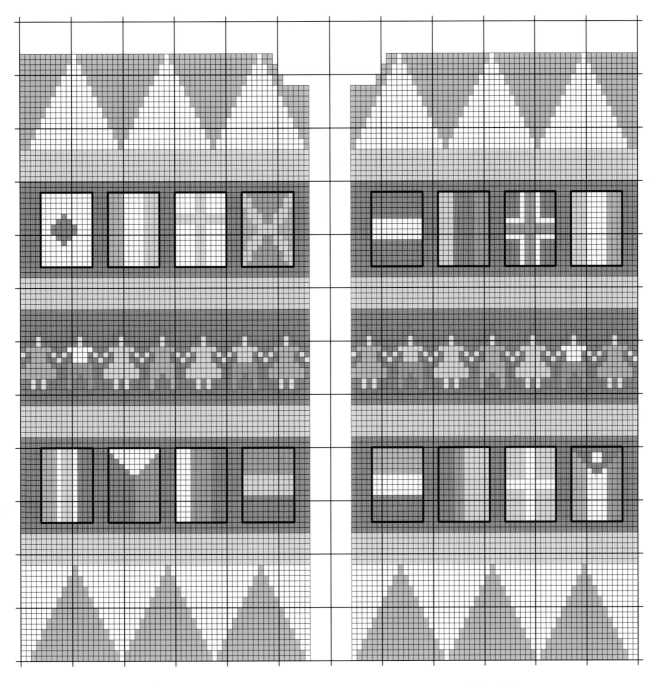

Chart B
Right Front

Chart C
Left Front

Permission granted to photocopy this page for your personal use.

Wings 'n Water
Cropped Kimono

INTERMEDIATE

SIZE: MEDIUM (LARGE)

FINISHED CHEST: 47" (49")

FINISHED LENGTH: 22" (23")

Inspired by an exquisite contemporary engraving, this swingy, cropped style is worked in ebony 100% cotton in reverse stockinette with stockinette verticals at wide intervals. The waterfowl and fish are also worked in cotton. Watery lines are surface-embroidered using a couching technique.

Fish and Fowl Details: Embroider as shown. For watery lines, lay out lines as shown, then couch them down with the yarn needle.

Lay down 2 strands Moss Green
and couch with 1 strand.

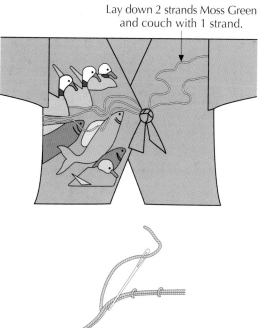

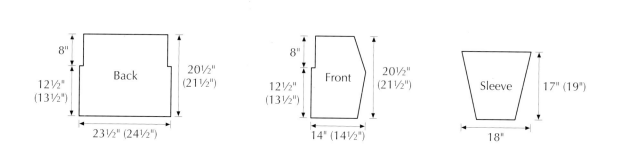

Couching

8"

12½"
(13½")

Back

20½"
(21½")

23½" (24½")

8"

12½"
(13½")

Front

20½"
(21½")

14" (14½")

Sleeve

17" (19")

18"

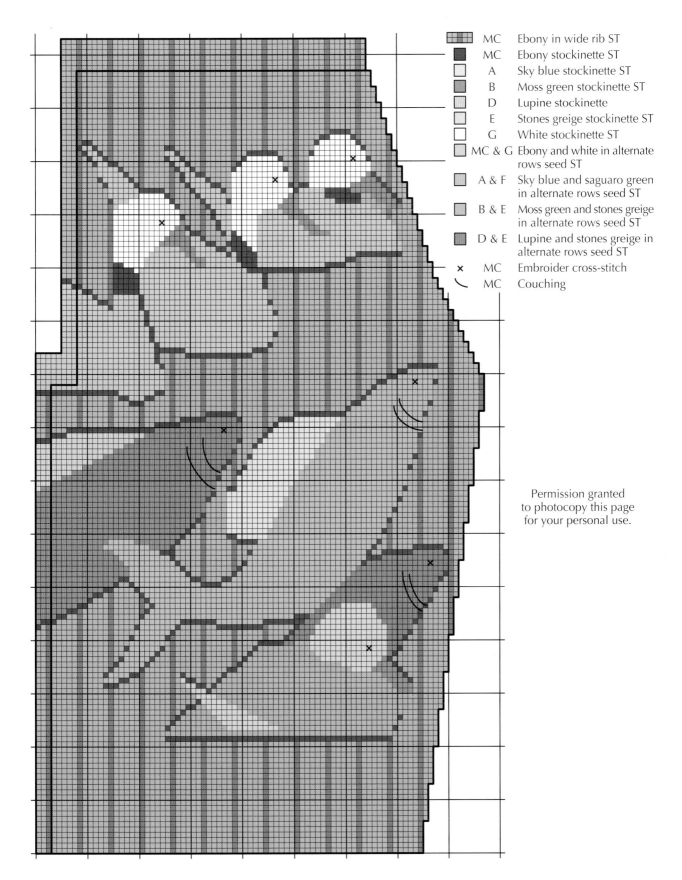

	MC	Ebony in wide rib ST
	MC	Ebony stockinette ST
	A	Sky blue stockinette ST
	B	Moss green stockinette ST
	D	Lupine stockinette
	E	Stones greige stockinette ST
	G	White stockinette ST
	MC & G	Ebony and white in alternate rows seed ST
	A & F	Sky blue and saguaro green in alternate rows seed ST
	B & E	Moss green and stones greige in alternate rows seed ST
	D & E	Lupine and stones greige in alternate rows seed ST
×	MC	Embroider cross-stitch
⟍	MC	Couching

Permission granted
to photocopy this page
for your personal use.

NORTHERN LIGHTS JACKET

INTERMEDIATE

ONE SIZE

FINISHED CHEST: 52"

FINISHED LENGTH: 29"

Slipstitch mosaic is easy color work. The colors of the aurora borealis on a late summer's evening in the northern islands are represented in this jacket. Rich blues and purples of the water, lit up at the horizon, become turquoise and lime. As the sunset mixes with the dazzling show of lights, rusty oranges and reds grow pinker before paling to delicate blues and lavenders.

MATERIALS

∾ 100-gram skeins (160 yards) of Hearty Worsted 100% Perendale Wool by Creative Yarns International

Color		No. of Skeins
MC	Magenta (as shown) or Brown Heather	11
A	Plum	1
B	Royal	1
C	Teal	1
D	Crystal	1
E	Seaspray	1
F	Burnt Orange	1
G	Ruby	1
H	Fuchsia	1
I	Violet	1
J	Hyacinth	1
K	Scot Mist	1
L	Celadon	1

∾ 50-gram skeins (110 yards) of Millie Mohair by Creative Yarns International

Color		No. of Skeins
M	Jade	1
N	Lime	1
O	Ruby	1
P	Fuchsia	1
Q	Hyacinth	1
R	Ice	1
S	Lilac	1

∾ US 10 needles or size to obtain correct gauge
∾ 5 stitch holders
∾ 7 buttons, 1" diameter

Gauge: 14 sts and 28 rows = 4" in Mosaic stitch on US 10 needles or size to obtain correct gauge

NOTE: *For Mosaic patterns, work in garter st, knitting 2 rows for each row of squares with color that begins row and slipping other squares.*

BACK

WITH MC, CO 106 sts. Work in K2, P2 ribbing for 8 rows, decreasing 1 st at end of last row. Knit 2 rows with A. Change to Wavelets Mosaic pattern and color sequence as follows, working 2 rows of each color as noted for Mosaic patterns. Alternate color stripes with MC.

Stripe	1	2	3	4	5	6	7	8	9	10
Color	B	A	B	A	B	C	B	C	B	C

Stripe	11	12	13	14	15	16	17	18	19	20	21
Color	M	C	M	D	M	D	M	D	E	D	E

Change to Sandrunners Mosaic pattern and continue color sequence as follows. Remember to alternate color stripes with MC.

Stripe	22	23	24	25	26	27	28	29	30	31
Color	N	F	O	G	O	G	H	P	H	P

Change to Aurora Mosaic pattern and continue color sequence as follows. Remember to alternate color stripes with MC.

Stripe	32	33	34	35	36	37	38	39	40	
Color	I	P	I	J	I	J	K	J	K	

Stripe	41	42	43	44	45	46	47	48	49	50
Color	J	Q	R	S	I	S	Q	L	I	Q

When piece measures 18" from beginning, BO 5 sts at start of next 2 rows. Decrease 1 st at each end of row every other row 7 times. Work even until armhole measures 11" in total length. Place remaining sts on holders.

POCKET LININGS

WITH LARGER needles and MC, CO 20 sts and work in St st for 4" or desired length. Place sts on holder. Make 2.

FRONTS

WITH MC, CO 51 sts. Work in K2, P2 ribbing for 8 rows. Knit 2 rows with A. Change to color sequences as for back. After #18, place center 20 sts on a holder and finish row. On next row, knit the pocket linings from the holders, sliding them onto left-hand needle and working them into pattern.

Continue, shaping armhole as for back, until piece measures 25" from beginning. Place 7 sts at center edge on holder, then decrease 1 st at neck edge every other row 4 times. Continue until front measures same as back in total length, then place remaining sts on holder. Make second front in same manner, but reverse shaping.

SLEEVES

WITH MC, CO 38 sts. Work in K2, P2 ribbing for 8 rows. Increase 12 sts on last row of ribbing. Knit 2 rows with A, then change to Wavelets Mosaic pattern in color sequence below, and continue, increasing 1 st at each end of every 6th row 12 times. As increases are made, add each new st to Mosaic pattern. Work even until piece measures 15½" in total length or desired length to underarm. Remember to alternate color stripes with MC.

Stripe	1	2	3	4	5	6	7	8	9	10	11	12
Color	B	A	B	A	B	C	B	C	B	C	M	C

Stripe	13	14	15	16	17	18	19	20	21	22	23	24
Color	M	D	M	D	E	D	E	D	E	D	G	H

SLEEVE CAPS

BO 5 sts at beginning of next 2 rows. Decrease 1 st at each end of row every other row 7 times. Continue, decreasing 1 st at each end of row every 4th row 8 times. To shape top of cap, BO 3 sts at beginning of next 10 rows. BO remaining sts. Remember to alternate color stripes with MC.

Stripe	1	2	3	4	5	6	7	8	9	10	11
Color	P	I	P	I	J	I	J	K	J	K	Q

Stripe	12	13	14	15
Color	K	Q	R	Q

FINISHING

REFER TO Basic Knitting Techniques on pages 6–8.

Knit shoulders together. Weave sleeve caps to armholes. Weave underarm seams.

Pocket: With smaller needles and MC, pick up sts from holder and work 4 rows of K2, P2 ribbing. BO and stitch down. Stitch down pocket linings.

Front Bands: With RS facing, smaller needles, and MC, pick up and knit along button side, skipping every 5th st as you go, for a total of approximately 144 sts. Work in K2, P2 ribbing for 8 rows. BO in pattern. Sew on buttons.

Repeat for buttonhole side, except on rows 4 and 5, work buttonholes opposite buttons as follows:

Row 4: Work sts to buttonhole place; *BO 2 sts, continue to next buttonhole place; repeat from * to end of row.

Row 5: Work sts to buttonhole place; *work 2 "e" wraps over bound-off sts, continue to next buttonhole place; repeat from * to end of row.

Collar: With RS facing, larger needles, and MC, knit sts from holder, then pick up and knit around neck, ending by knitting sts from other holder. Work back and forth in K2, P2 ribbing for 5" or desired length. BO loosely in ribbing.

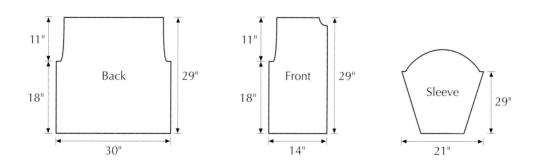

Sandrunners

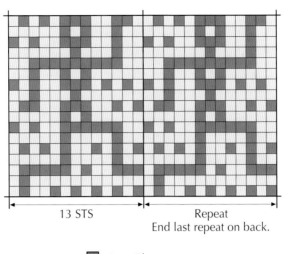

13 STS   Repeat
End last repeat on back.

- ▨ A   Plum
- ☐ CC   F G H N O P

Aurora

6 STS   Repeat

- ▨ MC   Magenta
- ☐ CC   I J K L P Q R S

Wavelets

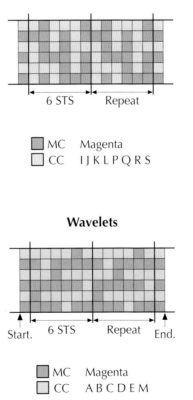

Start.   6 STS   Repeat   End.

- ▨ MC   Magenta
- ☐ CC   A B C D E M

EASY MOHAIR PULLOVER

BEGINNER

SIZE: SMALL (MEDIUM, LARGE)

FINISHED CHEST: 43" (45", 49")

FINISHED LENGTH

SHORT VERSION: 19" (19", 21")

LONG VERSION: 24½" (25½", 25½")

Make it long or short—this is a great shape and easy as pie.

MATERIALS

- 50-gram skeins (110 yards) of Millie Mohair by Creative Yarns International

  7 (7, 8) skeins for short version
  9 (9, 10) skeins for long version

- US 8 and US 10 needles or size to obtain correct gauge
- 4 stitch holders

Gauge: 14 sts and 18 rows = 4" in St st on US 10 needles or size to obtain correct gauge

BACK

WITH SMALLER needles, CO 76 (78, 86) sts. Work 4 rows in St st. Work in K2, P2 ribbing for 2". Change to larger needles and work in St st. Work even until piece measures 10" (10", 11") for short version or 15½" (16½", 16½") for long version. BO 3 sts at beginning of next 2 rows. Decrease 1 st at each end of every other row 4 times. Work even until piece measures 19" (19", 21") for short version or 24½" (25½", 25½") for long version. Place remaining sts on holder.

FRONT

WORK SAME as for back until piece measures 16" (16", 18") for short version, or 23" (24", 24") for long version. Place center 18 sts on a holder and, working both sides at once, decrease at neck edge 1 st every other row 3 times. When piece measures same length as back, place remaining sts on holders.

SLEEVES

WITH SMALLER needles, CO 28 (28, 32) sts. Work 4 rows in St st. Work in K2, P2 ribbing for 2". Change to larger needles and work in St st, increasing 1 st at each end of every 3rd row 18 times. Work even until piece measures 17½" (17½", 18½") from beginning. BO 3 sts at beginning of next 2 rows. Decrease 1 st at each end of next 16 rows. BO remaining sts.

FINISHING

REFER TO Basic Knitting Techniques on pages 6–8.

Knit shoulders together. Weave sleeve caps to armholes, easing into place. Weave underarm seams. With RS facing and smaller needles, pick up and knit around neck. Work in K2, P2 ribbing for 2¼", then work 4 rows St st. BO loosely in ribbing.

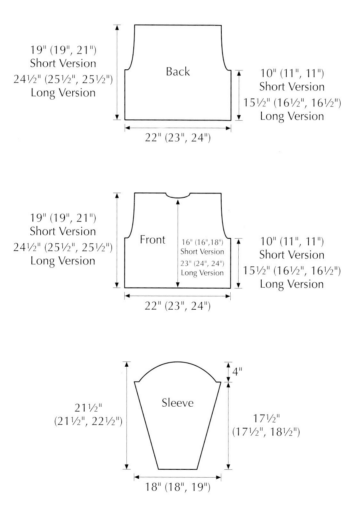

19" (19", 21")
Short Version
24½" (25½", 25½")
Long Version

Back

10" (11", 11")
Short Version
15½" (16½", 16½")
Long Version

22" (23", 24")

19" (19", 21")
Short Version
24½" (25½", 25½")
Long Version

Front

16" (16",18")
Short Version
23" (24", 24")
Long Version

10" (11", 11")
Short Version
15½" (16½", 16½")
Long Version

22" (23", 24")

21½"
(21½", 22½")

Sleeve

4"

17½"
(17½", 18½")

18" (18", 19")

CANYON GLOW WESKIT

INTERMEDIATE

SIZE: MEDIUM (LARGE)

FINISHED CHEST: 40" (44")

FINISHED LENGTH

BACK: 19½" (20¼") • FRONT: 22½" (24")

Women of the Great Lakes tribes often created panel bags, using a weft-twining weaving technique. Designs for these bags frequently depicted mythical images, such as the thunderbird with hourglass-shaped bodies.

MATERIALS

- 50-gram skeins (110 yards) of BioSpun Merino Wool by Creative Yarns International

Color		No. of Skeins
MC	Brown heather	5 (6)
CC	Natural	2

- US 3 and US 5 needles or size to obtain correct gauge
- US 3 circular needle (29") or size to obtain correct gauge
- 4 stitch holders
- 5 (6) small silver buttons

Gauge: 21 sts and 28 rows = 4" in St st on US 5 needles or size to obtain correct gauge

BACK

WITH SMALLER needles and MC, CO 100 (110) sts. Work in K1B, P1 ribbing for 5 rows. Increase 6 sts, evenly spaced across last row. Work from Chart A, shaping as shown. When all rows are complete, place remaining sts on holders.

POCKET LININGS

WITH LARGER needles and MC, CO 27 sts. Work in St st for 3". Place on a stitch holder. Make 2.

FRONTS

WITH LARGER needles and MC, CO 4 sts. Work from Chart B, increasing, binding off, and decreasing as shown. When decreasing for neck, use full-fashioned decreases (see page 6). Place 27 sts on holder, as indicated below thunderbird motifs, and place pocket linings on needle in their place; then continue in St st as before.

When working motifs, use separate bobbins of CC for each portion of wing, continuing with main ball of CC connected to body to produce smooth results. When all rows are complete, place remaining stitches on holders.

FINISHING

REFER TO Basic Knitting Techniques on pages 6–8.

Weave shoulders together. With RS facing, smaller needles, and MC, pick up and knit stitches around armhole, skipping every 5th st. Work in K1B, P1 ribbing for 4 rows. BO firmly. Weave underarm seams.

Pockets: With smaller needles and MC, pick up pocket sts from holders. Work in K1B, P1 ribbing for 4 rows. BO in ribbing. Tack down carefully to front side. Tack down pocket linings on back side.

Bands: With RS facing, smaller needles, and MC, pick up and knit all sts along bottom edge, marking center 2 sts of original 4 cast-on sts and last st before turning up center front edge. Pick up and knit along center front edge, skipping every 5th st; then pick up and knit along V, also skipping every 5th st (59 sts total); pick up and knit 42 sts across back of neck. Work second side same as first.

Work back and forth in K1B, P1 ribbing for 5 rows, except for 59 collar sts on either side of neck, which should be worked in seed st, working sts the opposite of what is facing you. Increase before and after markers on Rows 1 and 3. Also on Row 3, make 5(6) buttonholes on right side, spacing them approximately 10 sts apart as follows: YO; work 2 together for eyelet. On Row 4, pick up YO from previous row and work it as a st. After 5th row, BO all but sts on either side of neck, starting and ending where neck shaping begins and ends. Place these sts on holders.

Work collar on buttonhole side as follows:

Row 1: With RS facing, slip 1st st, P1, increase 1; work rest of row in seed st. (Work new sts into pattern each time.)

Row 2: Work even.

Repeat Rows 1 and 2, adding new sts to pattern until there are a total of 10 rows of seed st.

Rows 11–14: Work even in pattern.

Row 15: Slip 1, work 2 together, work to last 19 sts, turn.

Row 16: Slip 1, work even.

Row 17: Slip 1, work 2 together, work to last 38 sts, turn.

Row 18: Slip 1, work even.

Row 19: Slip 1, work 2 together, work 9 sts, turn.

Row 20: Slip 1, work even.

Row 21: Slip 1, work 2 together.

Row 22: BO in pattern.

Work collar on button side as follows:

Row 1: With RS facing, work in seed st to last st, increase 1, work 1. Work new sts into pattern each time.

Row 2: Slip 1, work even in pattern.

Repeat these 2 rows until 10 rows are complete.

Rows 11–14: Work even in pattern, continuing to slip 1st even-row st.

Row 15: Work to last 3 sts. Work 2 together, work 1.

Row 16: Slip 1, work to last 19 sts, turn.

Row 17: Slip 1, work to last 3 sts, work 2 together, work 1.

Row 18: Slip 1, work to last 38 sts, turn.

Row 19: Repeat Row 17.

Row 20: Slip 1, work 10 sts, turn.

Row 21: Repeat Row 17.

Row 22: BO in pattern.

Tack top of each collar piece to shoulder. Sew on buttons.

Back Belt: CO 6 sts. Knit every row for 13". Make 2. Tack to side seams just above waist. Overlap to pull in slightly at waist and tie.

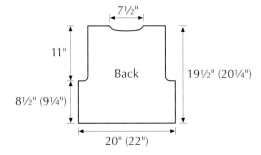

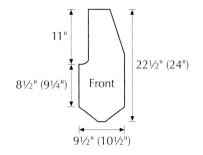

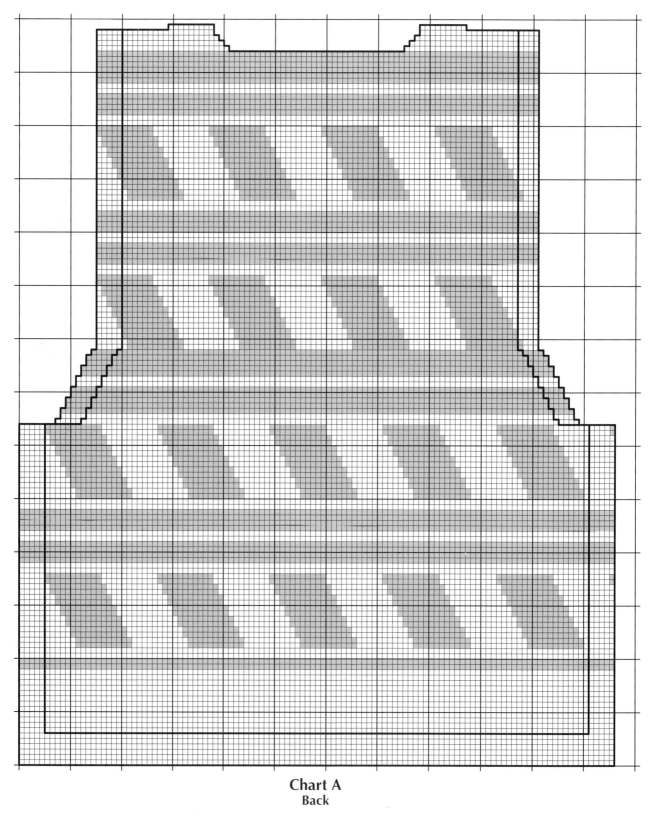

Chart A
Back

☐ MC   Brown Heather
☐ CC   Natural

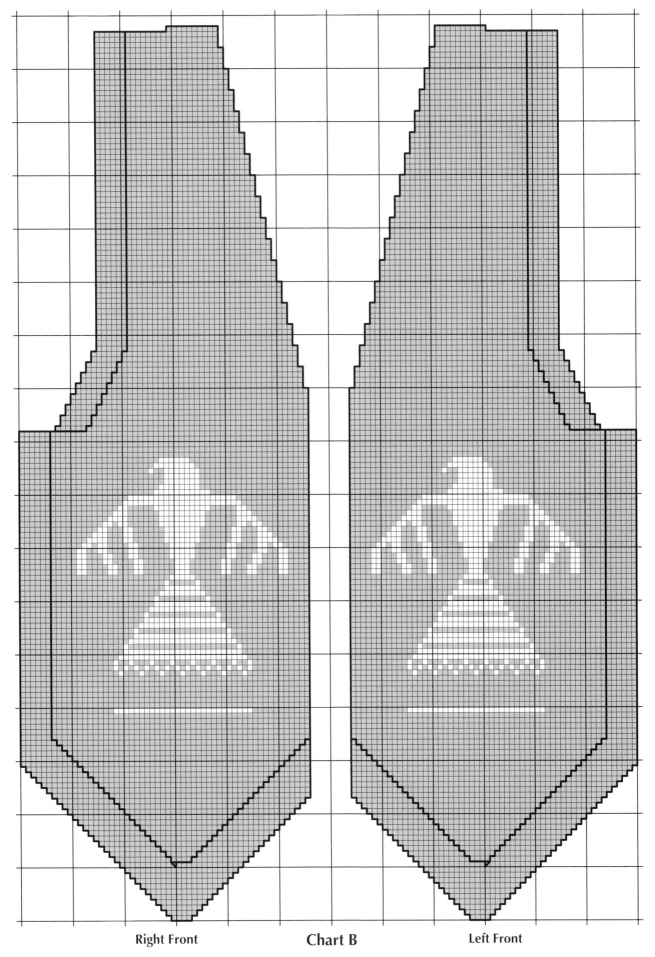

Right Front   **Chart B**   **Left Front**

BAMBOO KIMONO

INTERMEDIATE

ONE SIZE

FINISHED CHEST: 52"

FINISHED LENGTH: 27"

A wonderful decorative technique used by the Pueblos is incising, where grooves are drawn into clay in patterns. Here garter stitches and Entrelac (a change in stitch direction) are used to create the elegantly simple effect.

Pine Tree Guernsey

INTERMEDIATE

SIZE: SMALL (MEDIUM, LARGE)

FINISHED CHEST: 48" (50", 52")

FINISHED LENGTH: 27" (28", 29")

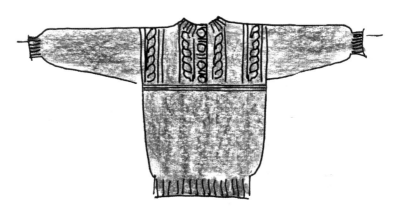

Make this comfortable pullover in the Guernsey tradition, with richly patterned stitch work on top and plain stockinette stitch on the lower portion.

BACK

WITH SMALLER needles, CO 110 (114, 120) sts and work in Cabled Rib for 6 repeats of Rows 1–4. Increase 10 sts across last row of ribbing. Change to larger needles and work in St st. Work even until piece measures 14" (15", 16") from beginning. End ready for a purl row. Place stitch markers at each end of needle for armholes. Knit 6 rows, increasing 2 sts evenly across last row with M1 increases (see page 7). Break yarn and slide sts back to start with right-side row. Begin pattern:

For size Small: K2, K1; work 55 sts in Pine Tree pattern; work 6 sts in Double Moss stitch; work 55 sts in Pine Tree pattern; K1, P2.

For size Medium: K2, P2, K1; work 55 sts in Pine Tree pattern; work 6 sts in Double Moss stitch; work 55 sts in Pine Tree pattern; K1, P2, K2.

For size Large: K2, P1, K1, P1, K1, P1, K1; work 55 sts in Pine Tree pattern; work 6 sts in Double Moss stitch; work 55 sts in Pine Tree pattern; K1, P1, K1, P1, K1, P1, K2.

Work even in pattern until Pine Tree pattern has been completed 3 times plus 18 rows more. BO center 36 sts. Continue in pattern, decreasing at neck edge every row twice. When piece measures 12" from beginning of 6 knit rows (garter band), place all sts on holders.

FRONT

WORK SAME as back until 6 rows of St st (after placing markers for armholes) have been completed, with increases at each end of last row.

For size Small: K2, K1; work 55 sts in Pine Tree pattern; K2.

For size Medium: K2, P2, K1; work 55 sts in Pine Tree pattern; K2.

For size Large: K2, P1, K1, P1, K1, P1, K1; work 55 sts in Pine Tree pattern; K2.

BO center 6 sts, then:

For size Small: K2, work 55 sts in Pine Tree pattern; K1, K2.

For size Medium: K2; work 55 sts in Pine Tree pattern; K1, P2, K2.

For size Large: K2; work 55 sts in Pine Tree pattern; K1, P1, K1, P1, K1, P1, K2.

Work both sides at once in established patterns, using a second ball of yarn and reversing sequence on other side until Pine Tree pattern has been completed 3 times plus 10 rows. On each side, place 12 center edge sts on holders. Continue in pattern, decreasing 1 st at neck edge every other row 5 times. Work even until piece is same length as back. Place remaining sts on holders.

SLEEVES

WITH SMALLER needles, CO 44 sts. Work in Cabled Rib for 2½". Change to larger needles and increase 16 sts across first row of St st. Continue in St st, increasing 1 st at each side of every 3rd row 30 times. Work even until sleeve measures 19" in total length. BO all sts *very loosely* with a needle 2 sizes larger. Work other sleeve in same manner.

FINISHING

REFER TO Basic Knitting Techniques on pages 6–8.

Knit shoulders together. With RS facing and smaller needles, pick up and work in pattern 12 sts from holder; then pick up and knit 20 sts along side of neck, 47 sts across back of neck, 20 sts along other side of neck; work 12 sts from other holder. Break yarn, and with RS facing, work in Cabled Rib as follows: K2, K1; *K2, P1, K1, P1; repeat from * 20 times, ending K1, K2. Work 12 rows of Cabled Rib. BO in pattern.

Front Placket: With RS facing and smaller needles, pick up and knit sts along front edge, including neck, skipping approximately every 5th st so that there are 46 sts on needle. Work 2 rows in K1, P1 ribbing, then work next row with buttonholes as follows: work 5 sts; *BO 2 sts, work 8 sts; repeat from *; work 2 sts. Next row: continue in pattern, working 2 "e" wraps over each bound-off st. Work even for 3 rows. BO. Work button side in same manner, but without buttonholes. Work 2 more rows. BO firmly. Sew on buttons.

Weave sleeves to body between markers. Weave underarm seams.

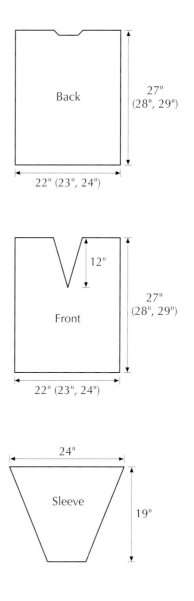

Yacht Club Cardigan

ADVANCED

ONE SIZE

FINISHED CHEST: 46"

FINISHED LENGTH: 24½"

The details on this great-fitting cardigan make it a pleasure to knit and to wear. A large cable forms the front band, and a dainty two-color rib makes a striking impression!

MATERIALS

- 50-gram skeins (109 yards) of 100% cotton

Color		No. of Skeins
MC	Taupe	10
A	Navy	6
B	Red	4

- US 3 and US 5 needles or size to obtain correct gauge
- Cable hook
- 7 stitch holders
- Stitch markers
- 7 small buttons

Gauge: 20 sts and 24 rows = 4" in St st on US 5 needles or size to obtain correct gauge

BRAIDED CABLE STITCH
(Multiple of 9 sts)

Rows 1, 3, 5, 7, 9, 11, 13: Knit 9 sts.
All even-numbered rows: Purl 9 sts.
Rows 5 and 15: Slip 3 sts to CN and hold at front of work, K3, bring sts on CN to back, K3, K3 from CN.
Repeat Rows 6–15 for pattern.

TWO-COLOR BABY CABLE RIB
(Multiple of 4 sts + 2)

NOTE: *When working this two-color ribbing, hold one color in each hand and use in turn, stretching your work sideways on your needle to avoid scrunching. This ribbing will not have elasticity, so this technique is very important.*

Row 1: P2 A; *K2 MC, P2 A; repeat from * across row.
Row 2: K2 A; *P2 MC, K2 A; repeat from * across row.
Row 3: P2 A; *skip 1st st of MC, knit into front of second st, then knit first st and drop both from needle, P2 A; repeat from * across row.
Row 4: Repeat Row 2.
Row 5: Repeat Row 1.
Row 6: Repeat Row 2.
Row 7: Repeat Row 3.
Repeat Rows 4–7 for pattern.

BACK

WITH SMALLER needles and Color A, CO 110 sts. Work in Two-Color Baby Cable Rib, using MC and A for 2½". Increase 5 sts, evenly spaced across last row of ribbing. Change to larger needles. Work from Chart A, using intarsia technique to change colors (see page 7). When Chart A is complete, change to MC and set up pattern as follows: K1, place a marker, K9 for Braided Cable, place a marker, K15, place a marker, K9 for Braided Cable, K19, place a marker, K9 for Braided Cable, place a marker, K19, place a marker, K9 for Braided Cable, place a marker, K15, place a marker, K9 for Braided Cable, place a marker, K1.

Continue in pattern, working single sts at each end in St st, Braided Cables where marked, and garter st for rest of sts until piece measures 10". Place all sts on holders.

FRONTS

WITH SMALLER needles and Color A, CO 54 sts. Starting right front with K3 in MC, and starting left front with P3 in A, work in Two-Color Baby Cable Rib for 2½", increasing 1 st at each end of last row. Change to larger needles and follow Chart B for right front and Chart C for left front. When charts are completed, change to MC and set up pattern as follows:

Right Front: K22, place a marker, K9 for Braided Cable, place a marker, K15, place a marker, K9 for Braided Cable, place a marker, K1.

Left Front: K1, place a marker, K9 for Braided Cable, place a marker, K15, place a marker, K9 for Braided Cable, place a marker, K22.

Continue in pattern, working single st at armhole edge in St st, Braided Cables where marked, and garter st for rest of sts until pieces measures 8". Place 12 sts at neck edge on a holder. Continue in pattern, decreasing 1 st at neck edge every other row 5 times. When fronts measure same as back, place remaining sts on holders.

SLEEVES

WITH SMALLER needles and Color A, CO 46 sts. Beginning and ending with P3 in A, work 2½" in Two-Color Baby Cable Rib. Increase 9 sts, evenly spaced across last row of ribbing. Change to larger needles and follow Chart D, working center 9 sts in Braided Cable in MC and increasing where indicated as follows: Work 1 st, increase 1, work to last st, increase 1 st, work last st.

When chart is completed, change to MC and set up pattern as follows:

K19, place a marker, K9 for Braided Cable, place a marker, K17, place a marker, K9 for Braided Cable, place a marker, K17, place a marker, K9 for Braided Cable, place a marker, K19.

Continue, working in garter st and Braided Cable as on front and back for 6" above chart work or desired sleeve length. BO all sts very loosely with a larger needle.

FINISHING

REFER TO Basic Knitting Techniques on pages 6–8.
Knit shoulders together. Weave sleeves to body above color work. Weave underarm seams.

Neckband: With RS facing, smaller needles, and MC, pick up and knit 88 sts around neck. Work in Two-Color Baby Cable Rib, starting with P2 in A for 1¼". Bind off firmly in A.

Front Bands: With smaller needles and A, CO 11 sts. Work in Braided Cable, slipping outside edge sts on each piece. On right front band, work eyelet buttonholes in center of every other braided cable as follows:

Row 9: K5, YO, K2tog, K4.

Row 10: Purl all sts, including YO from previous row.

Work until 7 buttonholes are completed. Work 4 more rows. BO, knitting sts 6 and 7 together as you go. Weave front bands to body. Sew on buttons.

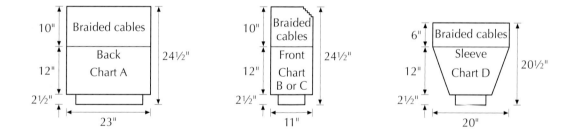

Chart A
Back

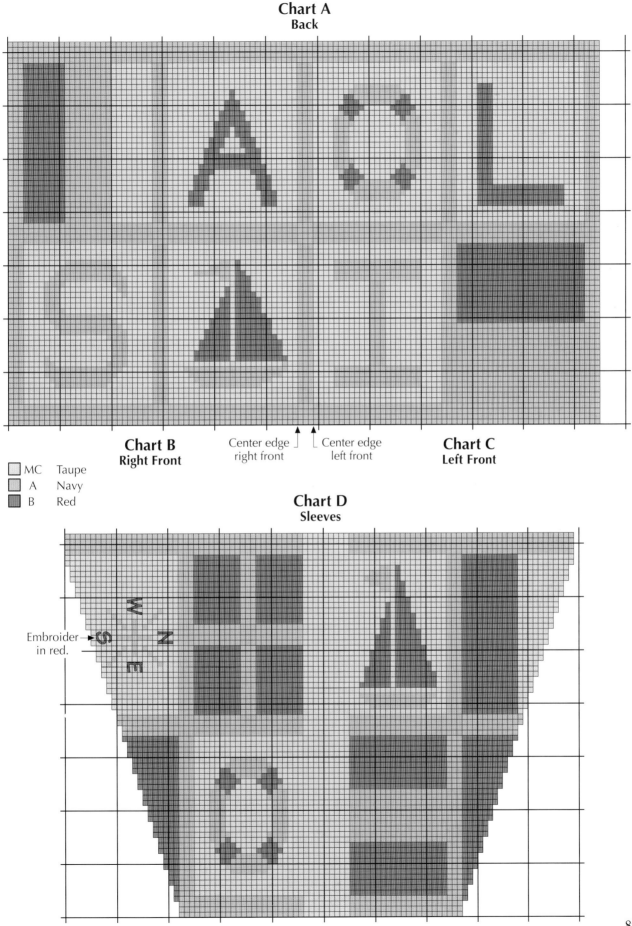

Chart B
Right Front

Center edge
right front

Center edge
left front

Chart C
Left Front

	MC	Taupe
	A	Navy
	B	Red

Chart D
Sleeves

Embroider → in red.

Permission granted to photocopy this page for your personal use.

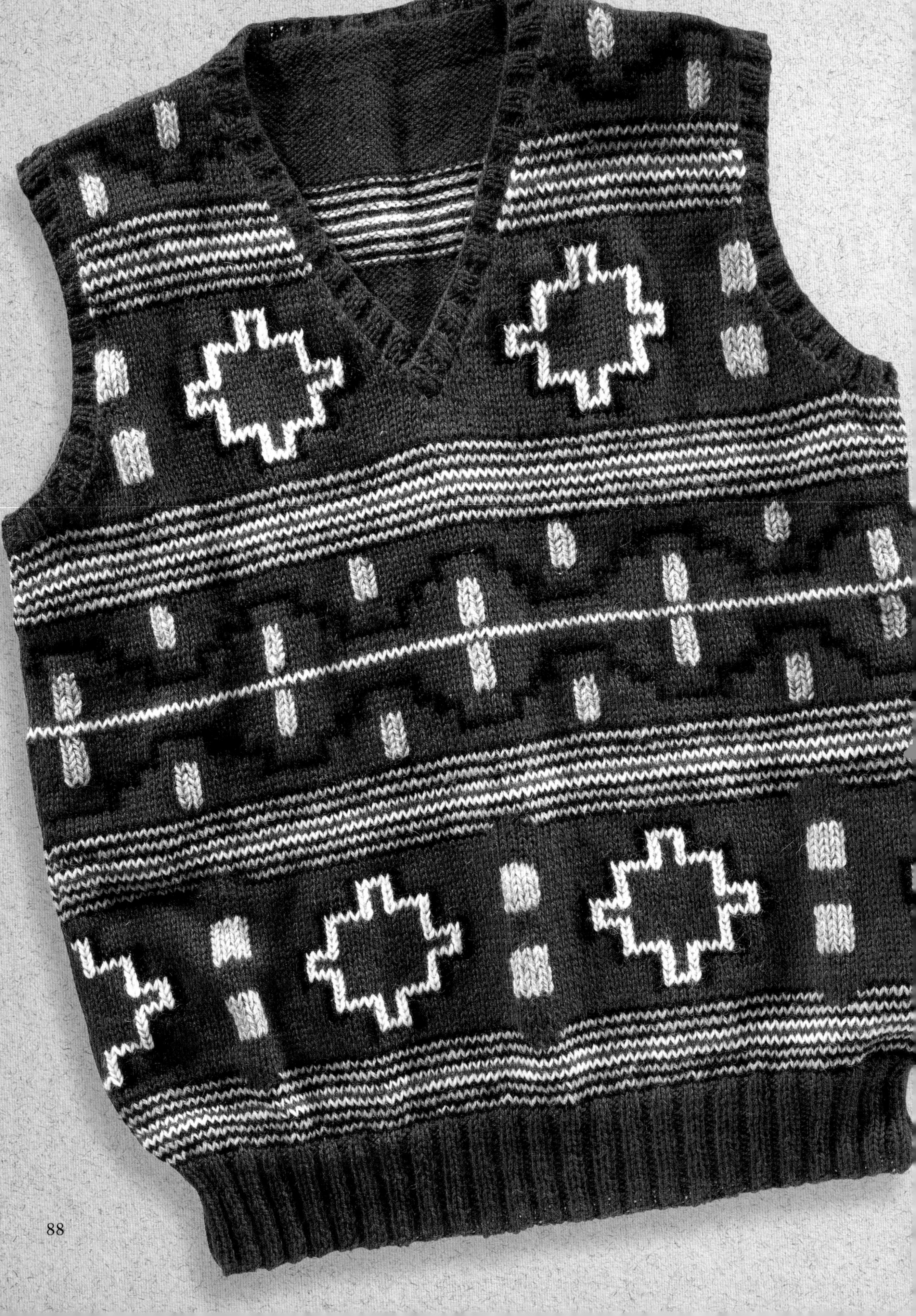

Men's Navajo Vest

INTERMEDIATE

SIZE: SMALL (MEDIUM, LARGE)

FINISHED CHEST: 42" (44", 46")

FINISHED LENGTH: 26¼" (26¼", 27¼")

This striking vest was inspired by a wonderful Navajo blanket. The colors and proportions of the stripes and motifs make it an enduring classic.

MATERIALS

50-gram skeins (110 yards) of DK-weight 100% wool

Color		No. of Skeins
MC	Red	4
A	Ebony	1
B	Greige	2
C	Natural	1

US 5 and US 7 needles or size to obtain correct gauge

Gauge: 20 sts and 26 rows = 4" in St st on US 7 needles or size to obtain correct gauge

BACK

WITH SMALLER needles and MC, CO 106 (110, 114) sts. Work in K2, P2 ribbing, beginning and ending with K2, for 2¾". Change to larger needles and work in St st, following chart for correct size and binding off and decreasing where shown.

FRONT

WORK SAME as for back, following chart for correct size with V-neck shaping. To make V-neck decreases, K1, K2tog TBL at beginning of row, and K2tog, K1 at end of row.

FINISHING

REFER TO Basic Knitting Techniques on pages 6–8. Weave shoulders together.

Neckband: Beginning at bottom of V-neck with RS facing, smaller needles, and MC, pick up and knit sts around neck, skipping every 6th st on front edges. Work back and forth in K2, P2 ribbing for ¾", then BO. Overlap at bottom and stitch down.

Armholes: With RS facing, smaller needles, and MC, pick up and knit sts around armholes, skipping every 6th st. Work in K2, P2 ribbing for ¾", then BO in ribbing. Weave underarm seams.

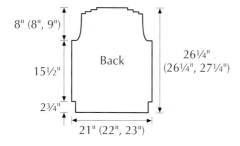

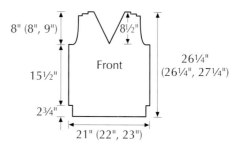

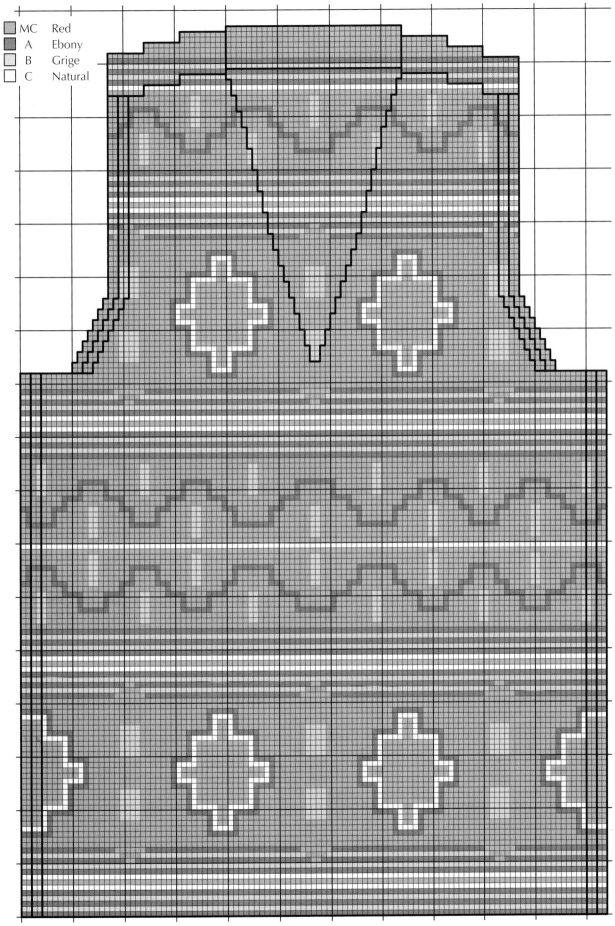

Back and Front

Permission granted to photocopy this page for your personal use.

Fisherman Vest

INTERMEDIATE

ONE SIZE

FINISHED CHEST: 46"

FINISHED LENGTH: 21"

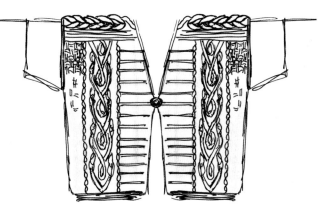

This little vest is sure to please. It's knit in one piece from the neck down. The strong character of the Interlocking Cable is contrasted with the delicacy of the Lacy Hearts Cable.

MATERIALS

- 50-gram skeins (109 yards) of 100% cotton

8 skeins

- US 3 and US 6 needles or size to obtain correct gauge
- Size E crochet hook
- Cable hook
- 1 large button, approximately 1" diameter

Gauge: 25 sts and 29 rows = 4" in combination of stitches on US 6 needles or size to obtain correct gauge

The stitches in this vest use the following abbreviations:

C2BW: Slip 1 st to CN and hold at back of work, P1, P1 from CN.

C4B: Slip 2 sts to CN and hold at back of work, K2, K2 from CN.

C4F: Slip 2 sts to CN and hold at front of work, K2, K2 from CN.

C6B: Slip 3 sts to CN and hold at back of work, K3, K3 from CN.

C6F: Slip 3 sts to CN and hold at front of work, K3, K3 from CN.

T2B: Slip 1 st to CN and hold at back of work, K1, P1 from CN.

T2F: Slip 1 st to CN and hold at front of work, P1, K1 from CN.

T3B: Slip 1 st to CN and hold at back of work, K2, P1 from CN.

T3F: Slip 2 sts to CN and hold at front of work, P1, K2 from CN.

T4B: Slip 2 sts to CN and hold at back of work, K2, P2 from CN.

T4F: Slip 2 sts to CN and hold at front of work, P2, K2 from CN.

INTERLOCKING CABLE *(Multiple of 6 sts + 9)*

Row 1: Knit.
Row 2: Purl.
Row 3: K3, *C6F; repeat from * to end of row.
Row 4: Purl.
Rows 5 and 6: Repeat Rows 1 and 2.
Row 7: *C6B; repeat from * to last 3 sts; K3.
Row 8: Purl.
Repeat these 8 rows for pattern.

DOUBLE SEED STITCH *(Multiple of 4 sts)*

On Right Side

Row 1: *K1, P1; repeat from * to end of row.
Row 2: Work sts as they face you.
Row 3: *P1, K1; repeat from * to end of row.
Row 4: Work sts as they face you.
Repeat these 4 rows for pattern.

On Left Side

Row 1: *P1, K1; repeat from * to end of row.
Row 2: Work sts as they face you.
Row 3: *K1, P1; repeat from * to end of row.
Row 4: Work sts as they face you.
Repeat these 4 rows for pattern.

MINI CABLE *(Multiple of 4 sts)*

Row 1: Knit 4.
Row 2: Purl 4.
Row 3: *C4F; repeat from * to end of row.
Row 4: Purl 4.
Repeat these 4 rows for pattern.

LACY HEARTS CABLE *(Multiple of 22 sts)*

Row 1: K1, P2, K1, P3, K2, P4, K2, P3, K1, P2, K1.
Row 2: Work sts as they face you.
Row 3: T2F, T2B, P3, T3F, P2, T3B, P3, T2F, T2B.
Row 4: K1, C2BW, K5, P2, K2, P2, K5, C2BW, K1.
Row 5: T2B, T2F, P4, T3F, T3B, P4, T2B, T2F.
Row 6: P1, K2, P1, K5, P4, K5, P1, K2, P1.
Row 7: K1, P2, K1, P5, C4B, P5, K1, P2, K1.
Row 8: Repeat Row 6.
Row 9: T2F, T2B, P3, C4B; C4F, P3, T2F, T2B.
Row 10: K1, C2BW, K4, P8, K4, C2BW, K1.
Row 11: P5, T4B, K4, T4F, P5.
Row 12: K5, P2, K2, P4, K2, P2, K5.
Row 13: P3, T4B, P2, C4B, P2, T4F, P3.
Row 14: K3, P2, K4, P4, K4, P2, K3.
Row 15: P1, T4B, P3, T3B, T3F, P3, T4F, P1.
Row 16: K1, P2, K5, P2, K2, P2, K5, P2, K1.
Row 17: T2B, T2F, P3, T3B, P2, T3F, P3, T2B, T2F.
Row 18: Work sts as they face you.
Repeat these 18 rows for pattern.

REGIMENTAL BARS *(Any multiple)*

Row 1: Knit.
Row 2: Purl.
Row 3: Knit.
Row 4: Purl.
Row 5: Knit.
Row 6: Knit.
Repeat these 6 rows for pattern.

BOBBLED DIAMONDS *(Multiple of 11 sts)*

This stitch uses the following abbreviation to indicate a Make Bobble:
Make Bobble (MB): (K1, P1) 3 times into same st, then pass 2nd, 3rd, 4th, 5th, and 6th sts over 1st st.

Row 1: P3, K2, MB, K2, P3.
Row 2: K3, P5, K3.
Row 3: P3, MB, K3, MB, P3.
Row 4: K3, P5, K3.
Rows 5 and 6: Repeat Rows 1 and 2.
Row 7: P2, T3B, P1, T3F, P2.
Row 8: K2, P2, K1, P1, K1, P2, K2.
Row 9: P1, T3B, K1, P1, K1, T3F, P1.
Row 10: K1, P3, K1, P1, K1, P3, K1.
Row 11: T3B, P1, (K1, P1) twice, T3F.
Row 12: P2, K1, (P1, K1) 3 times, P2.
Row 13: K3, P1, (K1, P1) twice, K3.
Row 14: Repeat Row 12.
Row 15: T3F, P1 (K1, P1) twice, T3B.
Row 16: Repeat Row 10.
Row 17: P1, T3F, K1, P1, K1, T3B, P1.
Row 18: Repeat Row 8.
Row 19: P2, T3F, P1, T3B, P2.
Row 20: K3, P5, K3.
Repeat these 20 rows for pattern.

SADDLE SHOULDERS

WITH LARGER needles, CO 25 sts. Set pattern for saddle shoulder as follows: K2, P1, K1, P1; work 15 sts in Interlocking Cable, then P1, K1, P1, K2. Continue in pattern, working sts other than cable as they face you in each row, for 9". BO all sts in pattern. Work other saddle shoulder in same manner.

BACK

WITH RS facing, pick up and knit 56 sts along side edge of first saddle shoulder piece, CO 25 sts across back of neck, then pick up and knit 56 sts across 2nd shoulder, for a total of 137 sts. Break yarn and restart on front side. Set pattern as follows: with RS facing, work 10 sts in Double Seed stitch, 4 sts in Mini Cable, P2, 22 sts in Lacy Hearts Cable, P2; work 4 sts in Mini Cable, 12 sts in Regimental Bars, 4 sts in Mini Cable, P3; work 11 sts in Bobbled Diamonds, P3, 4 sts in Mini Cable, 12 sts in Regimental Bars, 4 sts in Mini Cable, P2, 22 sts in Lacy Hearts Cable, P2, 4 sts in Mini Cable, 10 sts in Double Seed stitch (on left side). Work in established patterns until back measures 18" or desired length. With smaller needles, decrease 8 sts evenly spaced across first row; work 14 rows in garter st. BO all sts.

FRONTS

WITH RS facing and larger needles, pick up and knit 56 sts along the saddle shoulder edge between the 1st row of edge sts and the next row. Break yarn and start again on front side. Set pattern as follows: with RS facing, work 10 sts in Double Seed stitch, 4 sts in Mini Cable, P2, 22 sts in Lacy Hearts Cable, P2, 4 sts in Mini Cable, 12 sts in Regimental Bars. Work in reverse on other front at the same time. Work in established patterns, increasing at neck edge every 5th row 12 times. Work even until pieces measure 18", as on back. With smaller needles, decrease 4 sts evenly across first row; work 14 rows in garter st. BO all sts.

FINISHING

REFER TO Basic Knitting Techniques on pages 6–8.

Weave underarm seams, leaving 8" or desired armhole opening. Work 2 rows single crochet around neck and front edges. On 3rd and last row, make a button loop where shown at bottom of V by chaining 3, skipping 2 sts, then working a single crochet in 3rd st; complete row. Sew on button. Work 2 rows single crochet around each armhole, gathering cable sts together a bit on saddle shoulder.

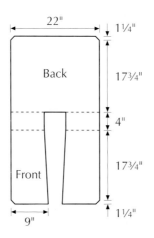